Relish
NORTH WEST

Original recipes from the region's
finest chefs and restaurants.
Introduction by Paul Heathcote, MBE.

First Published 2014
By Relish Publications
Shield Green Farm, Tritlington,
Northumberland, NE61 3DX.
Twitter: @Relish_Cookbook

ISBN: 978-0-9575370-6-4

Publisher: Duncan L Peters
General Manager: Teresa Peters
Design: Vicki Brown
Relish Photography: Tim Green, Kevin Gibson,
Nicky Rogerson and Andy Richardson
Editorial Consultant: Paul Robertson
Proofing Coordinator: Valerie McLeod
Sales: Wendy Rutterford
Coordinator: Rebecca Laycock

Front cover photograph by: Tim Green

Printed in China

OUR HAND PICKED RESTAURANTS

As the proud owner of a Relish cookbook, you may subscribe for your own personal Relish Rewards card which entitles you to free membership for one year.

You can access the Relish members' area on our website and find out what exclusive offers are available to you from the fantastic restaurants featured in our series of books throughout the UK.

SUBSCRIBE FOR YOUR REWARD CARD ON OUR HOMEPAGE
Simply register your name, address and title of Relish book purchased to receive your **FREE Relish Reward Card** **www.relishpublications.co.uk/relish-rewards**

When you make a reservation, simply let the restaurant know that you are a member and take your card along with you.

WHAT ARE THE REWARDS?
The rewards will continue to be updated on the website so do check and keep in touch. These range from a free bottle of Champagne to free gifts when you dine. Relish will send you a quarterly newsletter with special discounts, rewards and free recipes. We are about quality not quantity!

All offers are subject to change. See the Relish website for details.

www.relishpublications.co.uk/relish-rewards

004
CONTENTS

006
CONTENTS

Warm Summer Duck Salad with Lavender, Baby Gems and Crackling **Page 040**

009
STARTERS

020   Kidderton Ash Goat's Cheese Mousseline, Almond Purée, Port Jelly, Glazed Strawberries
030   Seared Scallops with Nori Salmon Roll
040   Warm Summer Duck Salad with Lavender, Baby Gems & Crackling
050   Shorthorn Beef Rib & Fillet, Wild Garlic Custard, Sumac, Onion & Malt Broth, Garden Herbs
060   Pla Salmon - Salmon Sashimi with a Lemongrass Salad
070   West Coast Crab Salad, 'Whippet Val's Curry', Apple, Mango
080   Goat's Cheese Three Ways (Snow, Beignet, Mousse), Roast Beetroot, Black Olive Wheel & Truffle Dressing
090   Twice Baked Lancashire Cheese Soufflé
100   Calamares Rellenos con Salsa Marinera - Stuffed Squid with Marinera Sauce
110   King Prawns with Samphire
120   Braised Saddleback Pork Cheeks, Parsnip Purée, Warm Mango & Roasted Cashew Nut Salad
130   Torbay Sole, Smoked Broccoli Purée, Mornay Bon Bons
140   Home Cured Salmon, Thai Crab Cakes, Pickled Vegetables, Wasabi Cream
150   British Wagyu Beef, Slow Cooked Egg Yolk, Rapeseed & Mustard Dressing
160   English Asparagus, Basil Oil, Quail Eggs, Balsamic Vinegar
170   Catalan Scouse
180   Black Pudding, Caramelised Apple, Sheeran's Brown Sauce
190   Citrus Cured Salmon, Sweet Pickled Fennel, Dill Mayonnaise, Cucumber & Lime Jelly
200   Pan Fried Red Mullet, Provençal Vegetables, Basil Oil, Tomato Vinaigrette
210   Risotto with Frogs' Legs, Crayfish, Snail, Nettles & Wild Garlic
220   Red Prawn, Mandarin Purée, Almond Crumb
230   Honey Roast Duck Salad, Confit Fritter with Orange & Ginger Dressing
240   Artichoke & White Tea Soup, Crispy Egg Yolk & Borage
250   Crab Mousse, Passion Fruit, Saffron Mayonnaise, Crab Rarebit
260   Liverpool Gin Cured Salmon, Cucumber Jelly, Gin & Tonic Jelly
270   Potted Crushed Chickpea, Apricot & Tamari Pâté, Cheese Shortbreads, Sesame Oat Biscuits
280   Rombo Arrosto - Roasted Turbot on Potato Pancake with Olives & Cherry Tomatoes
290   Cured Salmon, Potato Mousse, Baby Watercress, Pickled Beetroots
300   Veal, Baby Beetroot, Hazelnut
310   Duck Fritter, Yorkshire Rhubarb, Gingerbread
320   Goat's Cheese Panna Cotta, Candied Hazelnuts, Pickled Beetroot
330   Ravenglass Crab Cannelloni, Cucumber, Horseradish, Pickled Mackerel, Nasturtiums

Pan Seared Wild Sea Bass, Jersey Royal Gratin, English Asparagus With A Chive and Lemon Hollandaise **Page 232**

011
MAINS

022	Pan Fried Sea Trout, Heirloom Tomatoes, Samphire, Sweet Pea Liquor
032	Roast Goosnargh Duck Breast with Ricotta Gnocchi, Girolles, Peas, Beans & Asparagus
042	Wild Line Caught Liverpool Bay Sea Bass with Baby Vegetables & Keta Caviar
052	Turbot, Lemon Thyme Crumb, Leeks, Carrots, Chervil Gnocchi, Smoked Cod Roe & Chive Sauce
062	Penang Nua Yang - Fillet Steak with Rich 'Penang' Curry
072	Belted Galloway Beef, Blue Whinnow, Artichoke, Romanesco, Red Wine
082	Lune Valley Rack of Lamb, Herb Crust, Sweet Potato & Rich Port Jus
092	Roasted Rump of Lamb, Spring Vegetables, Jersey Royals
102	Carrillada De Cerdo - Ibérico Pork Cheek, Roasted Potatoes & Red Wine Jus
112	Smoked Duck Breast with Pomegranate & Chickpea Pilaf
122	Pan Fried Fillet of Monkfish, Herb Risotto, Crispy Parma Ham, Sweet Lemon Dressing
132	Braised Pork Neck, Caramelised Apple, Mini Roast Potatoes, Red & Green Cabbage, Crumbled Scratchings
142	Roast Local Grouse, Roast Roots, Spiced Pears, Bread Sauce
152	Brown Butter Poached Gigha Halibut, Baby Fennel, Pickled Pear & Jersey Royals
162	Yew Tree Farm Herdwick Hogget, Braised Breast, Rack, Heather, Broad Beans, Pancetta, Port Jus
172	Pluma Ibérica with Red Onion Chutney, Shallot & Beer Purée
182	Monkfish with Sesame, Saffron Potatoes, Summer Vegetables
192	Ballotine of Smoked 'Lords Lot' Pheasant, Toasted Pearl Barley, Artichoke & Blackberry Gastrique
202	Roast Fillet of Lancashire Beef, Smoked Bacon Lardons, Wild Mushrooms, Shallot Confit, Madeira Jus
212	Lake District Herdwick Lamb, Boulangère Potato, Confit Shoulder, Fennel Purée & Tapenade Jus
222	Chicken with Broad Bean Purée
232	Pan Seared Wild Sea Bass, Jersey Royal Gratin, English Asparagus with a Chive & Lemon Hollandaise
242	Pan Roast Brill, Pickled Vegetables, Pea Mousse, Garden Pea Salad, Anise Sauce
252	Maple Glazed Duck, Red Cabbage, Dauphinoise Potatoes, Orange Jelly, Golden Raisin Jus
262	Cod, Chorizo Pommes Anna, Sherry
272	Butternut Squash with Spiced Quinoa, Red Pepper Sauce & Hazelnuts
282	Filetto Di Manzo - Pan Seared Hereford Fillet of Beef, Rocket Pesto & Girolle Mushroom Sauté
292	Roast Breast of Gressingham Duck, Confit Leg Cannelloni, Celeriac Gratin, Duck Crackling, Sweet Potato Purée
302	Cod, Roast Leek, Pomegranate
312	Chicken Boudin, Smoked Pork Belly, Parisian Gnocchi, Asparagus, Wild Garlic
322	Gressingham Duck Breast, Granola, Raisin Purée, Yolk
332	Reg Johnson's Goosnargh Guinea Fowl, Pearl Barley, Hen of the Woods, Charred Baby Leeks, Spring Consommé

Deep Fried Jam Sandwich with Carnation Milk Ice Cream **Page 034**

013
DESSERTS

INTRODUCTION BY PAUL HEATHCOTE

My mother would say that, as a young boy, I was not the most adventurous when it came to food. Like most children, I recall not enjoying school meals but, at the age of 13, I do remember starting to take a greater interest in what my mother was baking and cooking. This interest led to my unusual request to join the girls in what was then called 'domestic science' - unlike the other boys being firmly held in woodwork or metalwork classes. After much persuasion, domestic science was eventually introduced for boys as an extra curriculum subject; I guess the school thought the novelty would soon fade away... it never did.

My stubborn northern traits, along with the curiosity and passion to learn, have served my career well. In later years, during apprenticeships at Sharrow Bay, The Connaught and Le Manoir, these attributes were probably the difference between being promoted, or a more talented commis beating me to it.

Of course, cooking is not all about hard work, graft and unwavering belief; successful kitchens are an unusual recipe. The desire to cook comes in many different forms; some chefs are great organisers, some are incredibly natural cooks, some are quiet and go about their daily business without fuss or hysterics, others are the very opposite - continually moaning or having an opinion about every delivery or dish served. What I do know is that the very best kitchens have all these ingredients and characters. I saw most of these qualities at the three great restaurants I worked in and the ones I own.

I saw how much love food can bring when my mother cooked for the family filling the room with joy and happiness. As for the school meals, it made me realise that, with a lot of hard work, curiosity and passion, all food could be so much better; after all, a braised piece of meat, a pie or a bowl of rice pudding can be exceptional in the right cook's hands.

When I returned to the North West in 1987, many described it as a culinary desert but it has changed beyond recognition. We have eating establishments, pubs, restaurants and cafes that can stand up to the best in the world. Chefs have influenced farmers and producers to grow and breed better. The determination to push boundaries, cook with passion and pride, take from the past and influence the future, makes these chefs and cooks stand out amongst their peers.

Take a drive from Hope Street in Liverpool to the wonderful countryside of Cumbria and the Ribble Valley and back into the City of Manchester and you will find the North West is blessed with famous chefs like Michael Caines, Paul Askew, Andrew Nutter and James Martin alongside many other establishments with great chefs and front of house managers.

I feel privileged to be introducing you to page after page of fantastic recipes from creative chefs in a variety of great places to eat, in a region where we are all so proud to work and is celebrated, right here, in Relish North West.

Paul Heathcote, MBE

016
1539

Nuns Road, Chester, CH1 2LY

01244 304 611
www.restaurant1539.co.uk Twitter: @Restaurant1539

Restaurant 1539 offers the most unique backdrop in which to enjoy a drink, savour a delicious meal or mingle on the Roof Lounge at the weekend.

The menu features some classic grills and fresh seafood, as well as an express menu, which includes a glass of wine for time-stretched diners at £9.95, available until 6pm Monday to Friday and until 4pm on Saturdays.

The weekend is the best time to indulge and enjoy food with friends. Open from 9.30am for breakfast, which is best accompanied by the Sunday papers, a bloody Mary to sooth a sore head or a glass of prosecco. A Sunday isn't complete without a delicious roast and we serve ours all day. It can be enjoyed with views over the famous racecourse.

1539's well stocked cellar boasts an impressive collection of Champagnes, wines and spirits, and the cocktail list is certainly worth exploring. The new layout of 1539 means that the bar is always ready to welcome passers-by, so it's the perfect place to meet friends for a catch up.

When the weekend arrives, unwind with drinks on the Roof Lounge where the atmosphere changes and a guest DJ transforms the ambience into a funky, sophisticated space to enjoy.

Restaurant 1539 is central to post race day celebrations at Chester Racecourse and, owing to demand, it is advisable to book early to avoid disappointment.

Relish Restaurant Rewards
See page 003 for details.

Restaurant 1539 is renowned for its quality of food, carefully selected by head chef Ian Penn. The inspired menu offers customers several twists on classic British favourites, alongside dishes inspired by flavours from across the globe. Penn has over 25 years fine dining experience at venues including Mayfair's 5 star Claridge's Hotel, The Park Lane Hilton in London and the Royal Automobile Club.

The restaurant has been accredited as the Best Large Restaurant in Cheshire and has been awarded with a Taste of Cheshire Award.

KIDDERTON ASH GOAT'S CHEESE MOUSSELINE, ALMOND PUREE, PORT JELLY, GLAZED STRAWBERRIES

SERVES 4

🍷 *Sauvignon Blanc, Nobilo 'Southern Rivers', East Coast (New Zealand)*

Ingredients

Mousseline

130g Kidderton Ash goat's cheese (rind removed)
150g firm cream cheese
50ml double cream

Almond Purée

1 small cauliflower
150g flaked almonds
250ml full-fat milk
25ml almond liquor

Port Jelly

200ml port
50g sugar
1.2g agar agar

Garnish

12 strawberries
caster sugar (to sprinkle)
50g peas
½ tsp mint (chopped)
½ tsp chives (chopped)
100ml extra virgin olive oil
micro herbs
deep fried vegetable crisps (crushed, for sprinkling)
4 red cherry tomatoes (*blanched* and peeled - see chef's tip)

shallow tray

Method

For The Mousseline

Beat the goat's cheese and cream cheese together. Add the cream, a little at a time and beat until smooth. Place in a piping bag and set to one side.

For The Almond Purée (Prepare the day before)

Shred the cauliflower, but ensure you don't use the root. Place in a pan with the almonds and milk. Bring to the boil and allow to simmer until the nuts are soft. Strain and keep the milk.

Blend the cauliflower and nuts until smooth, then add the almond liquor. If this is too firm add some of the reserved milk.

Allow to cool and refrigerate overnight. Place in a piping bag.

For The Port Jelly (Prepare the day before)

Bring the port and sugar to the boil. Add the agar agar and simmer for another 5 minutes. Pour into a shallow tray and chill overnight. Cut into even sized cubes, 1-1½cm square.

To Garnish

Slice the strawberries in half and sprinkle with caster sugar. Glaze with a kitchen blow torch or sear quickly in a hot pan. Mix the peas with the chopped mint. Season with salt and pepper, then finish with a drizzle of the olive oil.

Mix the chopped chives with the olive oil to make a thick dressing and season.

To Serve

Pipe 5 small mounds of goat's cheese mousse. Pipe 5 small mounds of almond purée. Add 3 diced jelly cubes and arrange 3 halves of strawberry. Scatter the peas and crushed vegetable crisps and plate the red cherry tomato with the micro herbs. Drizzle with the chive oil.

> **Chef's Tip**
>
> Remove the goat's cheese from the fridge 30 minutes before required so it is soft enough to pipe. *Blanch* the cherry tomatoes for 6-8 seconds and plunge into iced water. Peel the skin back gently and twist like a flame!

PAN FRIED SEA TROUT, HEIRLOOM TOMATOES, SAMPHIRE, SWEET PEA LIQUOR

SERVES 4

 *Gewürztraminer, Pirineos, Valdepenas
(Spain)*

Ingredients

4 x 160g sea trout (scaled and pin boned)

Tapenade

150g black pitted olives
1 clove garlic
4 anchovy fillets (in oil, not brine)

Pea Liquor

250g peas
150ml fish stock
25g butter

Tomatoes

2 yellow Heirloom tomatoes (roughly chopped)
2 green Heirloom tomatoes (roughly chopped)
2 orange Heirloom tomatoes (roughly chopped)
50g butter (diced)
200g samphire
5g chives (chopped)
100g micro watercress
1 tbsp basil cress
extra virgin olive oil (splash of)

Garnish

micro ruby mustard cress
micro chervil

Method

For The Tapenade

Blend all the ingredients together and set aside.

For The Pea Liquor

Bring the fish stock to a simmer in a pan with the butter.
Add the peas and cook for 2-3 minutes. Blend and pass through
a fine sieve. Season to taste.

> **Chef's Tip**
> Do not boil the pea liquor as this will turn it brown.

For The Tomatoes

Place the butter in a pan and gently melt it without colouring.
Add the tomatoes and allow to soften.

Add the samphire and, once softened, add the watercress.
Heat through until wilted, then add the chopped chives and
basil cress leaves. Finish with a dash of extra virgin olive oil.
Taste and season.

To Cook The Fish

Add a splash of oil to a non stick pan and bring to a medium
heat. Place the fish in the hot pan, skin-side down. Press the
fish down, as it will try to curl, for 30-40 seconds.

Once the flesh starts to change colour, turn over and cook
for a further minute. Remove from the heat and allow to finish
cooking using the residual heat in the pan.

Remove and drain onto a cloth.

To Serve

Arrange the tomato garnish onto the middle of a plate.
Place the fish on top. Drizzle with the pea liquor.

Finish with a teaspoon of tapenade on top of the fish.
Garnish with the micro leaves.

STRAWBERRY SCONE, STRAWBERRY JELLY, CLOTTED CREAM, CHAMPAGNE SOAKED GOLDEN RAISINS, SCONE CRUMB

SERVES 4

 Prosecco, Sant'O Rosa
(Italy)

Ingredients

Scone Crumb
125g self-raising flour
25g unsalted butter
75ml milk
20g sugar
1 egg (beaten, for brushing)

Strawberry Jelly
250g strawberries
100g caster sugar
120ml water
1g agar agar

Basil Sugar
20g fresh basil
100g sugar

Garnish
100g clotted cream
40g golden raisins (soaked in 50ml Champagne)
8 strawberries (quartered)
micro basil leaves

5cm cutter

Method

For The Scone Crumb

Preheat the oven to 220°C.

Lightly grease a baking sheet.

Mix the flour and salt together, then rub in the butter. Stir in the sugar and then the milk to get a soft dough. Turn out onto a floured work surface and knead very lightly.

Pat out to a round, 2cm thick. Use a 5cm cutter to stamp out rounds, then place on the baking sheet. Lightly knead together the rest of the dough and stamp out more scones to use up the dough.

Brush the tops of the scones with the beaten egg. Bake for 12-15 minutes until well risen and golden.

Allow to cool, then crumble into bite-sized pieces

For The Strawberry Jelly

Soften the strawberries with the caster sugar and water in a pan. Bring to the boil, add the agar agar and allow to simmer for 3 minutes.

Blend to a purée and pour into 4 dishes up to a quarter of the way up. Allow to cool in the fridge for 2-3 hours.

> **Chef's Tip**
> Use over-ripe soft strawberries to help create a sweet jelly.

For The Basil Sugar

Place the sugar and basil into a blender and blitz until green and fine.

Store in the freezer until needed.

To Serve

Evenly arrange the raisins over the 4 bowls of jelly. Spoon 3 teaspoon-size mounds of clotted cream onto each jelly. Arrange 8 pieces of the quartered strawberries and 3-4 pieces of the scone crumb. Finally, finish with micro basil leaves and the basil sugar.

026
60 HOPE STREET

60 Hope Street, Liverpool, L1 9BZ

0151 707 6060
www.60hopestreet.com

Renovated and transformed in 1999 by brothers Colin and Gary Manning, this family owned and run restaurant is a hive of culinary activity. 60 is spread over three floors of a Georgian town house in an area rich in history and wonderful architecture.

Award-winning for over a decade, the restaurant thrives on a changing menu of seasonal British produce. Now entering its 16th year, 60 Hope Street prides itself on its cuisine and service. Everything on the menu is created with the best quality, seasonal produce, all locally sourced with award-winning seafood from Southport, asparagus from Formby and lamb from Elwy Valley. 60's owners and their team are passionate and committed to providing the best standard of food delivered by an exceptional, unobtrusive level of service. Colin heads the front of house and writes the extensive 60 wine list, whilst Gary leads the way in the kitchen along with design and marketing.

The brothers' business philosophy underlies everything they do. "We started 60 because of our love for our city and our passion for food, especially local produce. We have been able to build strong relationships with small local suppliers and share our interests with our customers." says Colin.

60 offers a traditional, no-fuss approach, classic in style and accommodating to customers' needs. With a large and loyal following, the 60 Supper Club has developed, which enables guests to meet the producer whether that be a local food supplier, wine merchant or brewer.

Relish Restaurant Rewards
See page 003 for details.

It can be said that the Manning brothers, now with two sister restaurants to 60, are flying the flag high for their own city and for the North West, championing the great quality of what the area has to offer. Long may the flag fly!

SEARED SCALLOPS WITH NORI SALMON ROLL

SERVES 4

Albariño (Spain)
A wonderful aromatic white wine with fantastic acidity, especially great with seafood.

Ingredients

8 scallops (cleaned)
450g salmon (cut into 4 strips)
4 sheets nori seaweed
salt and pepper

Omelette

4 large eggs
4 spring onions finely sliced
2 tbsp sweet chilli sauce
salt and pepper
oil and butter (for frying)

Watercress Purée

140g watercress (*blanched*)
50ml warm vegetable stock
salt and pepper

Tempura Batter

100g cornflour
150g plain flour
10g baking powder
soda water (cold)

Method

For The Omelettes

Gently whisk the eggs with the sweet chilli sauce, then add spring onions. Season with salt and pepper. Over a medium heat, lightly oil a pan, add a knob of butter and fry 4 thin omelettes. Set aside to cool.

For The Watercress Purée

Blend the *blanched* watercress and warm stock together in a food processor to make the purée. Season to taste.

To Make The Nori Salmon Roll

Wrap a piece of seasoned salmon in the omelette, trimming off any excess. Wrap this tightly in the sheet of nori (this will self-seal). Repeat this with the remaining 3 slices of salmon.

For The Tempura Batter

Thoroughly combine all the dry ingredients together. Add the cold soda water, a little at a time, whisking gently to make a light batter. The batter should coat your finger.

To Serve

Dip each salmon roll in the tempura batter and deep fry (at 180°C) for 3½ minutes until crispy. Remove and drain well on kitchen paper. Cut each roll into 3 even pieces.

To cook the scallops, place in a lightly oiled frying pan on a medium heat and sear the scallops for 2 minutes on each side.

Swipe a spoonful of the watercress purée on the plate for the desired effect. Arrange the cooked scallops and salmon nori roll pieces on the plate as pictured.

> **Chef's Tip**
> Ensure the frying pan is hot to give a good colour to the seasoned scallops.

ROAST GOOSNARGH DUCK BREAST WITH RICOTTA GNOCCHI, GIROLLES, PEAS, BEANS & ASPARAGUS

SERVES 4

Pinot Noir (France)
A light to medium bodied red with rich fruit characters of red berry and cherry, soft with silky tannins.

Ingredients

4 duck breasts (trimmed, seasoned)

Vegetables

500g peas (podded, *blanched*)
12 spears asparagus (trimmed, halved)
100g Girolles (cleaned)
butter (good knob of)
salt and pepper

Gnocchi

50g butter
sea salt
200g fresh ricotta cheese
90g plain flour
3 egg yolks
½ nutmeg (grated)
150g Parmesan

Garnish

6 slices pancetta (oven dried until crispy)
red wine *jus* (optional)

10cm ring

Method

For The Duck

In a large frying pan, place the duck breasts, skin-side down, and cook on a low heat for approximately 8 minutes until the skin is crispy and the fat has rendered. Turn the breast over and cook for a further 5 minutes. Remove from the heat and allow to rest.

> **Chef's Tip**
>
> To cook the duck breast, start with a cold pan and place the duck skin-side down.

For The Mushrooms And Vegetables

On a low to medium heat, sweat off the Girolles with the butter in a *sauté* pan. When nearly cooked, add the peas and halved asparagus spears for a further 3-4 minutes until just cooked through. Season.

For The Gnocchi

Mix all the ingredients together in a large mixing bowl and make a dough. Roll out the dough on a lightly floured surface into cylinders approximately 3cm in diameter. Chill in the fridge until ready to use.

Remove the gnocchi dough and cut into 2cm pieces.

Just before serving, add a little oil and gently fry the gnocchi on each side for 2 minutes until golden brown.

To Serve

Place and layer the vegetables and Girolles with the gnocchi in a 10cm ring in the centre of the plate. Cut and dice the rested duck breast and arrange it around your plate. Garnish with the crispy pancetta. You may finish with a drizzle of red wine *jus*.

DEEP FRIED JAM SANDWICH WITH CARNATION MILK ICE CREAM

SERVES 4

 Muscat de Beaumes de Venise (France)
A light clear, golden dessert wine with floral
characters, honey and candied fruits.

Ingredients

Batter

10 whole eggs
750g self-raising flour
568ml full-fat milk
200g caster sugar

Strawberry Coulis

500g strawberries
100g icing sugar

Jam Sandwich

8 slices brioche (1cm thick)
1 x 340g jar strawberry jam
4 large strawberries (sliced)
icing sugar (to coat)
oil (for frying)

Carnation Milk Ice Cream

90ml double cream
210ml full-fat milk
75g caster sugar
150ml Carnation milk
4 large egg yolks

Garnish

10 strawberries (diced)
10 leaves mint (finely sliced)

Method

For The Batter

Whisk the eggs in a large mixing bowl until light and fluffy.
Sift in the flour and sugar mixing well, gradually adding the
milk, a little at a time. Combine the mix well between each
addition of milk to avoid lumps.

For The Coulis

Place the strawberries and icing sugar in a blender. Pulse to a
smooth paste. Pass through a fine sieve and chill.

For The Jam Sandwich

Spread the jam evenly on the brioche slices. Lay the sliced
strawberries on 4 of the slices then top with the remaining
brioche to form a sandwich. Dust heavily in icing sugar, making
sure all areas are covered to allow the batter to stick. Dip them
in the batter, being careful not to lose any of the filling. Gently
and carefully lower the sandwiches into the hot oil (180°C).
Cook each side until lightly brown on both sides. Remove from
the oil and drain on absorbent paper.

> **Chef's Tip**
> Use fresh, clean oil to cook the jam sandwich to ensure an
> even golden brown colour.

For The Carnation Milk Ice Cream

Bring the milk and cream to the boil then remove from the heat.

In a large mixing bowl, whisk the egg yolks and the sugar until
pale and creamy. Add the hot milk and cream mix and keep
whisking. Return to the pan and heat until it reaches 83°C.

Set aside to cool, add the Carnation milk and mix well. Churn
the mix in an ice cream machine until it sets.

To Serve

Scatter the diced strawberries on the plate, sprinkle over the
mint and drizzle with the strawberry coulis. Dust the sandwich
with icing sugar and slice to serve. The sandwich can be served
with fresh cream or the Carnation milk ice cream.

036
THE ART SCHOOL RESTAURANT

1 Sugnall Street, Liverpool, L7 7DX

0151 230 8600
www.theartschoolrestaurant.co.uk Twitter: @ArtSchoolLpool Facebook: artschoolrestaurant

Chef Paul Askew is a North West food champion and is recognised as one of the region's best chefs. For ten years, Paul was director of the highly acclaimed Hope Street Hotel and London Carriage Works Restaurant. He was invited to be a member of the Royal Academy of the Culinary Arts in 2006. His dream to open a fine dining food haven in Liverpool city centre was realised in 2014 with the launch of The Art School Restaurant, a high end, 50 cover fine dine restaurant and bar. Askew says, 'Any region, any great city, needs a culture of good food, and we have a restaurant scene that is developing at an incredible rate of knots'.

The Art School Restaurant is located in the stunning lantern room of the Victorian 1888 'Home for Destitute Children' building on Sugnall Street, and is merely a stone's throw away from Hope Street and Liverpool city centre. This area is one of the richest areas of the city in terms of culture and arts.

Paul is renowned for his passion for local produce and seasonal ingredients. He has been working with his chosen suppliers for many, many years and has therefore established close relationships where excellent quality is guaranteed.

Relish Restaurant Rewards
See page 003 for details.

By using only the finest produce and ingredients perfectly accompanied by superb wines and Champagnes, Paul will be reaching for the stars with the finest that Liverpool has to offer.

WARM SUMMER DUCK SALAD WITH LAVENDER, BABY GEMS & CRACKLING

SERVES 4

 Enjoy with a good chilled Pinot Noir or a Provence rosé

Ingredients

The Duck

2 large duck breasts
Maldon sea salt
1 tsp oriental five spice
1 tsp cracked black pepper
1 tsp liquorice powder
1 tsp lavender buds
3 cloves garlic (peeled)
50g butter

The Salad

½ punnet lambs lettuce
5 spring onions (washed, sliced)
½ orange (zest of, *julienned*)
½ head frisée lettuce (picked)
½ tbsp cider vinegar
1 tbsp olive oil

Warm Salad

1 baby gem lettuce (washed, outer leaves removed, cut into quarters)
5 or 6 radishes (washed, cut into quarters)
1 carrot (cut into ribbons)
200ml vegetable stock
vegetable oil

Raspberry Jus

200ml veal *jus*
½ punnet raspberries
½ tbsp cider vinegar

To Serve

1 tsp local honey
lavender flower

Method

For The Duck

Preheat the oven to 180°C.

Remove the skin from one of the duck breasts, season with salt, pepper and a pinch of five spice, then trap the skin between 2 sheets of silicon paper and 2 metal trays with a cast iron weight on top. Place in the oven for 5-7 minutes. While still hot, cut into pointed triangles. This makes a very moreish crackling. Retain the fat that comes off.

Grind the garlic, liquorice, lavender, salt, pepper and a little five spice with a pestle and mortar to make a punchy, fragrant rub. Rub this into the skinless and 'skin on' duck breasts ready for pan roasting.

Turn the oven down to 170°C. Heat the reserved duck fat in a non-stick heavy bottomed pan and seal the duck on both sides before adding some butter to baste. Finish in the oven for 2-3 minutes. Allow to rest thoroughly as the duck must be medium rare.

> **Chef's Tip**
> For your duck breasts, the more you rest, the more juices will be retained and the more tender it will be.

For The Salad

Combine the lambs lettuce, spring onions, orange zest, and frisée in a bowl. Dress with a little vinegar, oil and a little seasoning.

For The Raspberry Jus

Add the veal *jus* to a pan, crush in some raspberries, add a splash of vinegar for acidity and keep warm.

For The Warm Salad

Heat the baby gems, carrot ribbons and radishes in a pan with a little vegetable oil and seasoning. Allow them to wilt, but retain their crunch. Add the vegetable stock for moisture and steam to heat through.

To Serve

Before carving the duck and assembling as pictured, brush with local honey to add a glaze and sweetness. Carve in slices or chunky pieces and finish with the raspberry *jus*.

WILD LINE CAUGHT LIVERPOOL BAY SEA BASS WITH BABY VEGETABLES & KETA CAVIAR

SERVES 4

 Enjoy with a great glass of Bourgogne Blanc

Ingredients

Sea Bass

4 x 180g fillets of sea bass (descaled,
pin boned, salted)
4 oyster mushrooms
vegetable oil (for frying)
100g unsalted butter
lemon juice (spritz of)

The Sauce

25ml Noilly Prat
1 tbsp Chardonnay vinegar
1 shallot (finely diced)
1 bay leaf
100ml double cream
Maldon salt and white pepper (to season)
50g chives (chopped)

Baby Vegetables

4 baby Heritage carrots (peeled, *blanched*)
4 baby leeks (peeled, *blanched*)
300ml vegetable stock

Garnish

50g Keta caviar
2 sprigs chervil (picked)
lemon balm

Method

To Make The Sauce

Put the vinegar, Noilly Prat, shallot and bay leaf in a pan and
reduce by half, then add the cream and reduce again. Keep warm.

For The Baby Vegetables

In a saucepan, heat the vegetable stock ready to plunge the
vegetables into for reheating and finishing.

To Cook The Sea Bass

Heat a little vegetable oil in a non-stick frying pan and add
the salted fish, skin-side down. Press into the pan to make sure
full contact with the pan is made and there is no arching of
the bass. Add the oyster mushrooms to the pan, turn the fish
and add the butter for basting. The fish will be cooked after
3 minutes. Finish with lemon juice before serving.

To Serve

Add the chopped chives and seasoning to the sauce. Plate the
fish as per the photograph, on a bed of the baby vegetables.
Garnish with the Keta caviar, lemon balm and picked chervil.

> **Chef's Tip**
> A beautiful simple dish all about the freshness and quality
> of ingredients.

CLAREMONT FARM STRAWBERRY TART

SERVES 4

 Serve it with a great pink Champagne

Ingredients

Sweet Pastry

225g plain flour (sieved)
110g cold butter
80g caster sugar
1 large whole egg

Pastry Cream

350ml milk
4 egg yolks
65g caster sugar
15g plain flour
15g custard powder (or cornflour)
1 whole vanilla pod

Strawberry Glaze

4 strawberries
150g smooth apricot jam
4 tbsp water

To Finish

strawberries
icing sugar (to dust)

4 x 7cm individual tart tins

Method

For The Sweet Pastry

Rub the flour and cold butter together in a large bowl until a breadcrumb stage is reached.

Make a well in the centre of the flour mix and add the sugar, then the beaten egg.

Mix the dough using a metal spoon to prevent it from over mixing. Once it starts to come together, finish it by hand.

Leave the dough to rest in the fridge for 1 hour before rolling it out and lining your baking tins.

Preheat the oven 180ºC.

Lay a piece of good quality cling film over the top of the pastry and fill with baking beans. This will form a bag and stop any beans getting into your pastry. Bake in the oven for 10 minutes, remove the baking beans and return the tins to the oven to finish off until golden brown, approximately 8 minutes.

For The Pastry Cream

Whisk together the eggs and sugar in a large mixing bowl until they turn a pale gold colour. Whisk in the flour and cornflour. Set aside.

Place the milk and vanilla pod in a heavy bottomed pan. Bring to a gentle simmer, stirring frequently. Remove the pan from the heat and let it cool for 30 seconds.

Slowly pour half of the hot milk onto the egg mixture, whisking all the time, then return the mixture to the remaining milk in the pan. It is important to slowly pour the hot milk onto the cold eggs before you return the mixture to the pan to prevent the eggs from scrambling.

Bring the mixture back to the boil and simmer for 1 minute, whisking continuously, or until smooth.

Pour the cream into a clean bowl and dust with icing sugar to prevent a skin forming. Cool as quickly as possible by sitting the bowl of pastry cream in another larger bowl of iced water. Once cooled, refrigerate until needed.

For The Strawberry Glaze

Place all the ingredients in a pan and simmer for 5 minutes. Remove from the heat and blend with a hand blender to purée the strawberries.

Pass through a fine sieve into a pan. Make sure the glaze is hot before brushing over the fresh strawberries.

To Construct The Tart

Take your pastry case and fill with the pastry cream to about three quarters full, then decorate the top with fresh strawberries. Finally, brush the top with the hot glaze. To finish, dust with icing sugar.

046
ASKHAM HALL

Askham, Penrith, Cumbria, CA10 2PF

01931 712 350
www.askhamhall.co.uk Twitter: @AskhamHall

A stunning Grade 1 listed Pele Tower dating back to the late 1200s, Askham Hall has recently been transformed from a stately family home into a unique and contemporary stylish retreat and restaurant. Set in the unspoilt Eden Valley on the edge of the Lake District, a luxurious, intimate, unpretentious home from home awaits.

With modern furnishings and fresh decor, whilst carefully retaining the charm and character of this historic house, Askham Hall is somewhere you can relax in down to earth, comfortable surroundings. The antithesis of the traditional country house hotel, it is a bohemian-style retreat with a wonderful vegetable patch, fields and ponds with animals, set in the heart of an incredibly productive area for wild food.

The beautifully remodelled dining area is made up of three exquisite rooms and overseen by renowned chef Richard Swale, offering a unique and creative dining style using produce sourced from the surrounding fields and gardens and the 800-year-old family estate.
The cycle of life in the gardens and fields dictates the menus - they work with the seasons to grow, source and preserve the produce from the farms and woodland.

Continuing on from the success of their nearby sister establishment, the award-winning George and Dragon, Askham Hall promises a stunning menu.

Relish Restaurant Rewards
See page 003 for details.

Richard Swale grew up in Cumbria. He trained with John Burton Race and Anthony Demetre, before working in France. Richard has also undertaken placements around Europe which include Marc Veyrat and Noma. He works with gardener Colin Myers, who ensures an abundance of fresh seasonal produce. Completing the team is owner Charles Lowther, with his passion for livestock including Shorthorn cattle.

SHORTHORN BEEF RIB & FILLET, WILD GARLIC CUSTARD, SUMAC, ONION & MALT BROTH, GARDEN HERBS

SERVES 4

🍷 *Château Cos D'Estournel Saint Estèphe Bordeaux, 1989 (France)*

Ingredients

Rib

2kg beef rib bone
oil (for frying)
500g banana shallots (sliced)
4 cloves garlic
2 bay leaves
2 large sprigs thyme
1 litre red wine
2 litres white chicken stock

Wild Garlic Custard

300ml cream
3 eggs
120g wild garlic leaves
(juiced, reduced to 40ml)
40ml fresh wild garlic juice

Onion And Malt Broth

2kg white onions (sliced)
5 cloves garlic, 100g butter
2 litres fresh brown chicken stock
1 sprig thyme
4 leaves gelatine
malt extract (to season)
yeast extract (to season)

Roasted Silverskin Onions

20 silverskin onions (peeled, cut in half)
oil (for frying)

Raw Fillet And Sumac

12 thin slices beef fillet (like carpaccio)
sumac (pinch of) , salt (pinch of)

Garnish

fresh pea shoots, wild garlic flowers
micro radish leaves, allium flowers
micro coriander, Thai basil
broad bean flowers

Method

For The Rib

Heat some oil in a pan and colour the ribs. In another pan, sweat the shallots, garlic, bay leaves and thyme, add the wine and reduce until they are glossy. Add the chicken stock and reduce. Sieve the sauce and cool. Vacuum pack the beef ribs and the sauce and cook in a water bath at 65°C for 64 hours. Remove the ribs saving the sauce. Reduce the sauce. Remove the bones and trim the meat then cut into cubes. Glaze with the sauce until they are sticky. Alternatively, braise the ribs in the sauce in the oven at 130°C (fan) for about 4 hours or until the meat falls off the bone.

For The Wild Garlic Custard

Mix the ingredients and season. Cook in a *bain marie* at 140°C for 16 minutes until just set.

For The Onion And Malt Broth

Sweat the onions, garlic and butter, add the stock and thyme, allow to cool. Vacuum pack the broth. Fill a water bath, set to 62°C, add the broth bags and cook for 96 hours. Soak the gelatine leaves. Strain the broth, bring to the boil and add the gelatine leaves. Once cooled, freeze in a container. Remove the broth, wrap in a muslin cloth and hang over a container so the mixture drips off. Season with malt and yeast extract. Alternatively, you could cook the onions and stock in a pan for 1 hour, then strain and finish with the malt and yeast extract.

Roasted Silverskin Onions

Preheat the oven to 170°C (fan).
In an ovenproof pan, fry the onions, flat side down, in a little oil. Transfer to the oven for 5 minutes or until cooked.

For The Raw Fillet And Sumac

Season the beef fillet with the sumac. The hot broth will cook the fillet.

To Serve

Place the beef fillet on the plate and dot around with the wild garlic custard. Add the rib cubes and roasted silverskin onions. Garnish with fresh pea shoots, wild garlic flowers, micro radish leaves, allium flowers, micro coriander, Thai basil and broad bean flowers. Pour over the hot broth and serve the garlic custard on the side.

Chef's Tip

Once you have picked the fresh herbs, place straight into ice cold water to refresh them and stop them from wilting.

TURBOT, LEMON THYME CRUMB, LEEKS, CARROTS, CHERVIL GNOCCHI, SMOKED COD ROE & CHIVE SAUCE

SERVES 4

 Chassagne Montrachet Premier Cru Morgeot
Fernand et Laurent Pillot, Burgundy, 2012 (France)

Ingredients

Fish
4 turbot fillets
butter (to fry), lemon juice (spritz of)

Smoked Cod Roe And Chive Sauce
400g banana shallots (sliced)
3 cloves garlic (sliced)
butter (knob of)
sprig thyme, bay leaf
400ml white wine
1 litre good quality fish stock
250ml double cream, 20g chives
25g smoked cod roe (or to taste)

Chervil Gnocchi
2 Maris Piper potatoes
60g Parmesan (grated)
2 egg yolks
2 tbsp fresh chervil (chopped)
125g plain flour

Braised Leeks
4 young leeks (trimmed to 10cm)
250ml fresh chicken stock
chervil (handful of), chives (handful of)

Baby Carrots
8 baby carrots
thyme, bay leaf, butter (knob of)
1 tsp sugar, salt (pinch of)

Leek Purée
3 leeks (white part only, finely diced)
butter (knob of), spinach (handful of)
200ml cream

Lemon Thyme Crumb
200g butter (soft)
2 tbsp lemon thyme (chopped)
4 tbsp Panko breadcrumbs

Method

For The Smoked Cod Roe And Chive Sauce
In a pan, sweat the shallots and garlic, with the butter for about 10 minutes. Add the thyme, bay leaf and wine then reduce by two thirds. Add the fish stock and again reduce by two thirds. Add the cream and reduce until sauce consistency. Pass through a sieve, then put the sauce in a blender with the chives and cod roe. Once blended, pass through a fine sieve once again. Set aside.

For The Chervil Gnocchi
Boil the potatoes until just cooked, dry off and pass through a sieve. Whilst warm, add the Parmesan, egg yolks and chervil, then knead in the flour. Roll out into long sausages. Cut into 2cm pieces and poach in boiling water. Once they float to the top, refresh in iced water. Set aside.

For The Braised Young Leeks
Braise the leeks in the stock with the chervil and chives. Season with salt and cook for about 10 minutes until tender.

To Cook The Baby Carrots
Place all the ingredients in a pan and cover with water. Slowly cook the carrots until just cooked. Keep in the liquid until ready to serve.

For The Leek Purée
On a low heat, sweat the leeks in the butter until translucent. Add the cream and cook for another 10 minutes. Add the spinach, cook for 1 minute, then blend in a blender until smooth. Pass through a fine sieve and reserve.

To Make The Lemon Thyme Crumb
Mix the butter and lemon thyme together. Fry the breadcrumbs in 2 tablespoons of lemon thyme butter until lightly golden brown. Season with salt and set aside.

To Serve
Season the turbot and grill on a low heat. Fry the gnocchi in butter until golden brown. Heat the leeks and carrots in their own cooking liquid. Warm the sauce and purée. When the fish is cooked, season with a little lemon juice. Arrange all ingredients artistically on the plate. Sprinkle a spoon of the thyme crumb on the fish and serve.

> **Chef's Tip**
> Always season your fish and meat just before frying, not in advance, as this draws moisture out of the flesh which will stop it caramelising properly.

RHUBARB & PISTACHIO DESSERT, GREEK YOGHURT SORBET

SERVES 8-10

 Terroirs des Châteaux Fort Rolly Gassmann Alsace, 2011 (France)

Ingredients

Pistachio Crumble

100g butter (diced)
100g sugar
160g plain flour
20g pistachio paste (chopped - not too fine)
50g pistachio nuts

Pistachio Cake

4 eggs
200g sugar
1½ oranges (zest of)
25g pistachio paste
50g blended pistachio nuts
25g plain flour
50g ground almonds
50g fresh white breadcrumbs
1½ tsp baking powder
200ml vegetable oil

Pistachio Panna Cotta

225ml double cream
225ml milk
40g sugar
40g roasted pistachios
20g pistachio paste
3 gelatine leaves (soaked in cold water)

Rhubarb Pieces, Strips And Purée

125g sugar
200ml water
few drops grenadine (for colour)
10 juniper berries
5 medium sticks rhubarb (trimmed)

Greek Yoghurt Sorbet

300ml Greek yoghurt
50g sugar, 150ml water
sorbet stabiliser

25x35cm baking tray
(lined with greaseproof paper)

Method

For The Pistachio Crumble

Preheat the oven to 160°C (fan).

In a bowl, crumble all the ingredients together with your fingertips. Place on parchment paper on a tray, spread out evenly and bake in the oven for 20 minutes. Once cooked, leave to cool, then break it down into crumbly pieces.

Pistachio Cake

Preheat the oven to 180°C (fan).

Whisk the eggs, sugar, orange zest and pistachio paste in the mixer until light and fluffy. In a bowl, mix together all the other dry ingredients. Pour the vegetable oil into the egg mixture, whilst still whisking, then mix all the dry ingredients into the egg mixture. Pour into your prepared tray. It will sit about 2½cm thick. Bake for 25 minutes.

For The Pistachio Panna Cotta

Add all the ingredients, except the gelatine, into a pan and bring to the boil, whisking to break up the pistachio paste. Remove from the heat, squeeze the water out of the gelatine and add to the mixture. Infuse for 20 minutes. Pass through a fine sieve and set in a container. Decorate with the rhubarb strips if you wish.

For The Rhubarb Pieces, Strips and Purée

Bring the sugar, water, grenadine and juniper berries to the boil and set aside.

For the strips: Using a vegetable peeler, peel a few strips of rhubarb. Take half of the sugar liquid, bring to the boil and drop the strips in the liquid. Remove from the heat and set aside. For the batons: Place the rhubarb in a vacuum pack bag, add the rest of the liquid, seal in a vacuum machine and cook in a water bath at 85°C for 10 minutes, or until just tender. Once cooked, refresh in iced water then open the bags and cut the batons into the desired size. Alternatively, poach gently in the liquid until just tender. Blend the rhubarb trimmings in a blender to form a purée.

To Make The Greek Yoghurt Sorbet

Dissolve the sugar in the water, cool, then combine all the ingredients. Place in a paco jet container, freeze and churn when needed. Alternatively, churn in an ice cream machine and freeze.

To Serve

Serve as pictured.

> **Chef's Tip**
> Rhubarb is ready to be picked when the leaves go from wrinkly to flat.

056
CHILLI BANANA THAI RESTAURANT

71 WaterLane, Wilmslow, Cheshire, SK9 5BQ

01625 539 100
www.chillibanana.co.uk

The authentic taste of Chilli Banana's Thai home cooking has built a strong following since the original award-winning restaurant opened in Wilmslow in 1996.

Their delicately flavoured traditional dishes are inspired by evening banquets that executive chef May Wakefield's family enjoyed as she grew up in Thailand's Prachinburi Province. It's part of the whole passion for Thai food and culture that underpins the Chilli Banana reputation.

"The best Thai food is a way of sharing the values of our farming family and saying 'this is Thailand'," says May.

Hand-picked Thai chefs at Chilli Banana's Wilmslow and Liverpool restaurants, specialise in family recipes from a combination of imported Asian ingredients and fresh locally farmed produce. Their exotically unfamiliar regional dishes such as Laab Moo Pa, a north eastern Thai salad of wild boar, toasted rice grains, dried chilli and mint, Gung Ob Wun Sen, prawns and vermicelli steamed in a pot with fresh ginger and herbs or Pla Song Kreuang, a lightly fried sea bass served topped with crunchy, fresh mango salad are not adapted to suit western tastes. They are the real thing. Cooked and served with a passion for traditional home cooking - the way it's done in Thailand.

Entry to Chilli Banana's stylish new two-storey town centre restaurant, on the corner of Water Lane, is through an atrium of Thai lanterns into a dining room overlooking a state-of-the-art open kitchen. Three thousand handmade bricks were shipped from Ayutthaya in the Chaophraya valley and Thai furnishings, art and decorations came 6,000 miles by container ship to guarantee a genuine Asian experience.

Relish Restaurant Rewards
See page 003 for details.

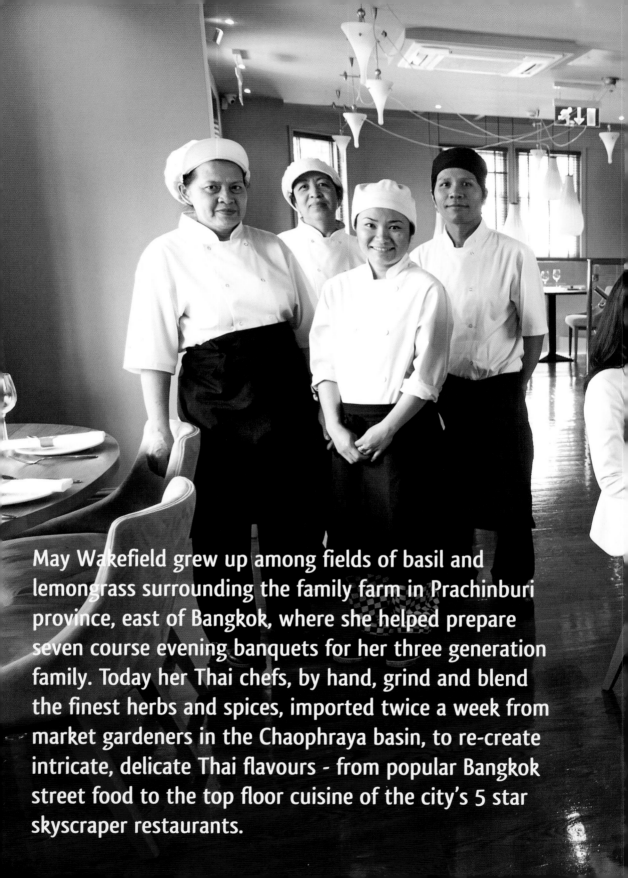

May Wakefield grew up among fields of basil and lemongrass surrounding the family farm in Prachinburi province, east of Bangkok, where she helped prepare seven course evening banquets for her three generation family. Today her Thai chefs, by hand, grind and blend the finest herbs and spices, imported twice a week from market gardeners in the Chaophraya basin, to re-create intricate, delicate Thai flavours - from popular Bangkok street food to the top floor cuisine of the city's 5 star skyscraper restaurants.

PLA SALMON
SALMON SASHIMI WITH A
LEMONGRASS SALAD

SERVES 1

🍷 *Turckheim Gewurztraminer*
(France)

Ingredients

60g sashimi grade salmon loin (thinly sliced)

Chilli Oil

3 tbsp good quality cooking oil
1 heaped tsp chilli flakes

Lemongrass Salad

1 tbsp lemongrass (finely sliced)
1 tbsp ginger (shredded lengthways)
1 tbsp spring onions (thinly sliced)
1 tbsp red onion or shallot (thinly sliced)
1-2 kaffir lime leaves
¼-½ tbsp chilli oil
1 tbsp nam pla (fish sauce)
¼-½ tbsp freshly squeezed lime juice
1 tsp sugar
3-4 mint leaves
1 fresh small chilli (finely chopped, optional)

Method

For The Chilli Oil (Prepare ahead)

Heat the oil in a frying pan on a medium heat. When the oil is medium hot, not smoking, add the chilli flakes. Stir the chilli in the oil for a few seconds, then turn off the heat. Continue to stir for a few minutes, then leave to cool naturally. Store in a sterilised jar.

For The Lemongrass Salad

Mix all the ingredients together except the fresh chilli. Taste and add the fresh chilli if required.

To Serve

Place the salad on the serving plate with the thinly sliced salmon on top or to the side.

> **Chef's Tip**
>
> Always use the best sashimi grade salmon for this uncooked salmon dish.
>
> To ensure the best flavours, chop the salad ingredients shortly before mixing them. You can use shop bought chilli oil which can be found in most oriental supermarkets or from online suppliers. Try to find one with a smooth taste.

PENANG NUA YANG
FILLET STEAK WITH RICH 'PENANG' CURRY

SERVES 2

 *Franschhoek Semillon
(South Africa)*

Ingredients

The Paste

½ tsp coriander seeds
½ tsp fennel seeds
15 dried long red chillies (chopped)
2 medium stalks lemongrass (trimmed,
finely chopped)
2 tsp kaffir lime fruit rind (finely chopped)
1 tbsp shrimp paste
9 medium cloves garlic (peeled)
3cm length fresh galangal (finely chopped)
4 medium shallots (chopped)

The Curry

200-250g fillet steak (about 2½cm thick)
2 tsp cooking oil
2 tbsp penang curry paste
1 tin good quality coconut milk
2 tbsp sugar
2 tbsp nam pla (fish sauce)

Garnish

2 kaffir lime leaves (cut into strips)
red chilli (sliced)

Method

For The Paste (Makes about 7 tablespoons of paste)

Gently roast the coriander and fennel seeds in a dry frying pan, being careful not to burn them. This will release the flavours. Grind the roasted seeds into a powder using a large stone mortar and pestle. Add the remaining ingredients, then pound to form a smooth paste. This will take some time. Alternatively use an electric grinder. With this method a little water will need to be added.

For The Curry

Heat a ribbed iron pan under the grill. When hot, grill the steak, turning once. We cook it as medium rare. Set aside to rest.

At the same time, in a well-ventilated room, heat the oil in a wok on a medium heat and fry the curry paste, breaking it up to mix into the heated oil. Cook for a further few seconds. This will produce a pungent aroma. Slowly add the coconut little by little, mixing all the time. When all the coconut milk has been added and combined, season with the sugar and fish sauce.

To Serve

Slice the steak into 1cm slices. Arrange on a heated serving plate and dot the curry sauce at the side. Sprinkle with the kaffir limes leaves and sliced chilli.

This rich and flavoursome dish can be served in its own right with steamed Thai fragrant rice or eaten as part of a communal meal along with a selection of salad, stir fry, vegetables and rice.

Chef's Tip

This dish is made in 2 stages. First making the curry paste and then the curry.

Penang curry paste can be bought in oriental supermarkets or from online suppliers but you can't beat a freshly made curry paste. Unused paste can be portioned and frozen.

KOW NEOW MAMMUANG
MANGO WITH SWEET STICKY RICE

SERVES 2

 Freshly brewed jasmine or green tea

Ingredients

Sticky Rice
110g glutinous rice
water (to cover)
110ml tinned coconut milk
3 tbsp sugar
¼ tsp salt

1 large, ripe, sweet mango

Garnish
½ tsp sesame seeds (roasted)
edible flowers

Method

To Cook The Rice (Using a steamer)
Cover the sticky rice with water and soak for at least 2-3 hours in a bowl. Ideally, leave to soak overnight as my mum would do.

Set up your steamer with enough water in the bottom to steam for around 20 minutes. Cover the basket or trivet with a muslin cloth and pour in the soaked rice. Put the lid on and steam for around 10 minutes, boiling the water on a high heat. Turn the rice over and continue steaming for a further 10 minutes. When cooked, the rice will turn translucent. At this point remove it from the heat.

To Cook The Rice (Using a microwave)
Cover the sticky rice with water and soak for 10 minutes in a bowl. The water level should be just over the rice.

Cover the bowl with a small plate and heat in the microwave on full heat for 2½ minutes. Stir the rice and return to the microwave for a further 2½ minutes. Stir again and cook for another 2 minutes. The rice grains should now be translucent.

> **Chef's Tip**
> It's easy to tell when sticky rice is cooked as it turns translucent.

For The Sweet Coconut Milk
Whilst the sticky rice is cooking, bring the coconut milk to a gentle simmer in a saucepan and stir in the sugar and salt. Remove from the heat.

As soon as the sticky rice is cooked, spoon the sweetened coconut milk over the rice, mixing it in really well to coat all the grains of rice. Cover and leave to stand for 10 minutes. Keep a few spoons of coconut milk for the topping.

To Prepare The Mango
Peel the mango, then slide your knife closely down each side of the stone to give 2 good sized pieces. Slice each piece and arrange on separate plates.

To Serve
Divide the sticky rice into 2 and place next to the mango. Spoon over the remaining coconut milk, sprinkle over a few sesame seeds and decorate with the edible flowers.

066
THE COTTAGE IN THE WOOD RESTAURANT WITH ROOMS

Magic Hill, Whinlatter Forest Park, Keswick, Cumbria, CA12 5TW

01768 778 409
www.thecottageinthewood.co.uk Twitter: @Cottage_In_Wood

Located in the heart of Whinlatter, England's only Mountain Forest, and just five miles from the bustling market town of Keswick, The Cottage in the Wood is a 17th Century coaching inn that has been lovingly restored. 'The Cottage' provides a tranquil and relaxing ambience and is the perfect base for exploring the north western fells of the Lakes. Ideally situated between the Lakes of Bassenthwaite, Derwentwater, Buttermere, Crummock Water and Loweswater, the area is great for walking, cycling, sailing, golf and a host of adventure activities.

The restaurant provides stunning views of the mighty Skiddaw mountain range and the surrounding forest. The area provides a rich larder; Herdwick hogget from the surrounding fells, freshly landed fish and shellfish from Whitehaven harbour and a host of wild foods, many foraged from within the forest. The quality of the food, wine and boutique accommodation has won The Cottage several regional and national awards, gaining recognition in the leading guides.

Head chef Chris Archer has been passionate about cooking since childhood. Aged 14, his school work experience was at the Michelin starred Vineyard at Stockcross with head chef John Campbell. His apprenticeship under chef Germaine Schwab at Wintergham Fields instilled into him traditional techniques and methods. Chris is nonetheless receptive to new trends and, whilst keeping his nose to the grindstone, always has an eye on the horizon.

Relish Restaurant Rewards
See page 003 for details.

Any awards and accolades are history - we're about looking to the future and raising the bar continually. That's it.

WEST COAST CRAB SALAD, 'WHIPPET VAL'S CURRY', APPLE, MANGO

SERVES 4

 Pinot Gris, Andre Thomas (Alsace, France)

Ingredients

Crab Salad
200g picked white crab meat
2 tbsp mayonnaise
2 tbsp thick natural yoghurt
½ stick celery (finely *brunoise*)
½ Granny Smith apple (skin on, finely *brunoise*)
20 coriander leaves (*julienne*)
2 limes (juice of)

Whippet Val's Curry Purée
2 onions (finely sliced)
1 garlic clove (finely sliced)
oil and butter (for frying)
½ tbsp curry powder
½ tsp ground ginger
½ tsp ground cinnamon
¼ tsp plain flour
1 tsp tomato purée
570ml beef stock
½ tbsp Branston pickle

Mango Purée
4 ripe mangoes (peeled, cut into small dice)
1 tsp caster sugar, 1 lime (juice of), 50ml water

Curry Oil
1 tsp curry powder, 1 tsp coriander seeds
1 tsp cumin seeds, 1 tsp turmeric powder
100ml vegetable oil

Cauliflower Beignets
12 cauliflower florets (size of little fingernail)
plain flour (to dust)
1 egg (beaten), 100g breadcrumbs

Pickled Apple
100ml white wine vinegar
100ml white wine, 100g sugar
1 Granny Smith apple

Garnish
coriander cress

Method

For Whippet Val's Curry Purée
In a pan, slowly cook the onions and garlic, without colouring, in the oil and butter until soft. Stir in the spices and flour and cook out for 30 seconds. Add the pickle and tomato purée then stir in thoroughly.

Slowly add the stock, a ladle at a time, stirring constantly to create a smooth sauce. Simmer the sauce for 30 minutes, or until the liquid has almost all gone. Blend to a purée. Check the seasoning and store in a squeezy bottle.

For The Mango Purée
Place all the ingredients into a heavy bottomed pan, cover and cook over a low heat until the mango is totally soft and begins to go mushy. Blitz until smooth. Pass through a sieve and store in a squeezy bottle.

For The Curry Oil (Prepare the day before)
Gently toast the spices in a dry pan over a low heat until aromatic. Tip the spices into a clean pan and cover with the oil. Leave to infuse overnight. Pass through a fine sieve. Store in a squeezy bottle.

For The Cauliflower Beignets
Blanch the florets in boiling, salted water for 30 seconds. Refresh in iced water. Drain on a cloth to dry the florets. Dust in a little flour, coat in beaten egg then toss through the breadcrumbs.

For The Pickled Apple (Prepare ahead)
Place the white wine vinegar, sugar and white wine into a pan. Bring to the boil, then allow to cool. Core the apple and slice horizontally on a *mandolin* to achieve thin discs. When the liquor is cool, add the apple slices and leave to pickle for 2 hours.

For The Crab Salad
Thoroughly combine all the ingredients and check for seasoning. Store in the fridge until needed.

> **Chef's Tip**
> Be sure to pick through the crab meat before mixing to check for any shell.

To Assemble
Arrange a ring of mango purée in the centre of the plate. Fill the mango with a pile of crab salad, then top with a disc of pickled apple. Pipe 3 large and 3 small dots of the curry purée around the contour of the plate.

Deep fry the cauliflower beignets at 180°C for 1 minute until golden and crispy, then drain on paper and place on the small dots of curry. Drizzle some curry oil around and garnish with coriander cress.

BELTED GALLOWAY BEEF, BLUE WHINNOW, ARTICHOKE, ROMANESCO, RED WINE

SERVES 4

 Felton Road, Bannockburn Pinot Noir
(New Zealand)

Ingredients

Beef And Braised Beef

1 whole rib cap (taken from the top of the ribeye)
500g piece ribeye steak
½ bottle good red wine
1 litre chicken stock

Red Wine Sauce

5 shallots (sliced)
10 button mushrooms
3 cloves garlic
1 sprig thyme
1 bottle red wine
braising liquor from the beef
2 litres veal stock

Caper And Raisin Purée

250g raisins
250g capers (rinsed in cold water to remove brine)

Braised Artichokes

12 violet artichokes
1 litre white chicken stock
200ml white wine vinegar
250ml olive oil
sprig thyme
sprig parsley
1 clove garlic
pinch salt
¼ tsp each coriander seeds, fennel seeds and cumin seeds

Garnish

12 Cavolo Nero cabbage leaves
12 Romanesco cauliflower florets
4 slices Blue Whinnow cheese
1 pear (skin on, cut into 12 slices)

Chef's Tip
Use a metal skewer to check the core temperature of the ribeye. Hold against your top lip, it should feel warm for a medium rare-medium cuit!

Method

For The Beef (Prepare the day before)
Remove the rib cap from the top of the ribeye and trim well. Remove the sinew from the eye of the meat and split vertically down the middle.

Wrap each piece of ribeye tightly in plenty of cling film to form a cylinder. Set in the fridge until needed.

Fry the rib cap on both sides in a hot pan until deeply caramelised. Remove the meat and *deglaze* the pan with red wine. Place the beef in a casserole dish deep enough to hold all the remaining ingredients. Cover with a lid and braise in the oven at 150°C for 6 hours. When tender, remove from the liquor and press between 2 trays in the fridge overnight. Pass the liquor through a sieve.

For The Red Wine Sauce
Sauté the shallots and mushrooms in a large casserole pan until golden. Add the garlic and thyme, followed by the red wine. Reduce the wine by half, then add both stocks. Simmer over a low heat, skimming regularly, until a rich sauce consistency is achieved. Strain the sauce through a *chinois*.

For The Caper And Raisin Purée
Place the raisins and capers in a pan and cover with water. Simmer over a low heat until the water has fully evaporated. Blend until smooth. Store in a squeezy bottle.

For The Artichokes
Place all the ingredients, except the artichokes, in a pan and bring to a simmer.

Peel the artichokes with a knife. Following the contours of the stalk, run the knife down and over the heart, removing all of the green outer leaves. Add the artichokes to the simmering liquid and cook for 10 minutes. Leave to cool in the liquor. Slice in half and remove the hairy choke from the middle. Return to the liquor until needed.

To Finish
Cut the ribeye into even sized steaks, season with salt and pepper then caramelise on all sides. Place the steaks in the oven at 60°C for 15 minutes.

Cut the rib cap into 8 cubes and warm through in some of the red wine sauce, basting constantly.

Blanch the vegetables separately, toss in melted butter and season with salt.

Slice the ribeye in half and season with a little rock salt. Plate with the cut side up, arrange the other elements of the dish as per the photograph, finally pouring on the sauce and garnishing with the cheese and pear.

ARCTIC ROLL, FIG, PISTACHIO, GREEN TEA, LIME

SERVES 8

 Tokaji 5 Puttonyos (Hungary)

Ingredients

Fig Purée
250g dried figs
200ml port
200ml red wine
30ml balsamic vinegar

Fig Parfait
2 egg yolks
15g honey
15g sugar
150g fig purée
190ml cream (lightly whipped)

Arctic Roll Sponge
2 whole eggs
2 egg yolks
115g ground almonds
10g cornflour
130g caster sugar (plus more to dust)

Pistachio Sorbet
850ml milk
60ml water
150g glucose, 150g sugar
150g pistachio paste

Green Tea And Lime Syrup
125g sugar, 125ml water
2 green tea bags
1 lime (juice of)

Green Tea Meringue
125g green tea syrup (cold)
5g egg white powder

Lime Jelly
125g green tea and lime syrup
25ml lime juice
1½ leaves gelatine (soaked in water)

To Serve
pistachios (crushed)

50x30cm silpat mat or tray
(lined with baking parchment)

Method

Chef's Tip
Prepare all elements of this dish the day before. Place your knife in a pan of hot water before cutting the arctic roll to ensure a smooth slice.

For The Fig Purée
Place all the ingredients in a pan, cover with a *cartouche* and cook until the liquid has reduced. Blend until smooth and pass through a fine sieve.

For The Fig Parfait
Whisk the yolks, sugar and honey over a *bain marie* until it thickens to 'ribbon stage'.
Stir in the fig purée, then fold in the lightly whipped cream. Roll in cling film to form a cylinder, approximately 45mm in diameter and 20cm long. Freeze for 6 hours.

For The Arctic Roll Sponge
Preheat the oven to 160°C.
Blitz all the ingredients in a food processor until smooth.
Pour onto the silpat mat and bake for 8 minutes, until set but not coloured. Remove from the oven, dust with caster sugar and cover with greaseproof paper. Carefully release from the silpat mat and turn out.
Spread some fig purée onto the sponge and wrap around the parfait. Tightly wrap in cling film to accentuate the cylindrical shape. Return to the freezer.

For The Pistachio Sorbet
Warm the milk. Place the remaining ingredients into a separate pan and bring to the boil, stirring continuously. Cook out until slightly thick. Blend the milk and pistachio mix together. Cool, churn in an ice cream machine and freeze.

For The Green Tea And Lime Syrup
Dissolve the sugar in the water and bring to the boil. Remove from the heat and add the tea bags and lime juice. Strain.

For The Green Tea Meringue (Prepare the day before)
Whisk the ingredients until a soft meringue forms. Pipe small meringues onto a lined tray and allow to dry overnight in a warm oven (50°C).

For The Lime Jelly
Warm the syrup and add the gelatine to dissolve. Add the lime juice and set in a shallow container in the fridge for 2 hours.

To Assemble
Cut a nice thick slice of the arctic roll and place on one side of the plate. Using a paintbrush, swipe a little of the fig purée along the opposite side of the plate to the arctic roll. Alternating, place 3 meringues and 3 spoons of jelly along the purée. Finish with a scoop of pistachio sorbet and garnish with crushed pistachios.

CRAGWOOD COUNTRY HOUSE HOTEL

Windermere, Cumbria, LA23 1LQ

01539 488 177
www.cragwoodhotel.co.uk Twitter: @LDCHotels

Cragwood Country House Hotel is situated idyllically in the heart of the Lake District. Located on the shores of Lake Windermere with over half a mile of our own lake frontage, Cragwood enjoys gorgeous views over the lake and surrounding Lakeland fells. Set in a secluded, 20 acre estate of beautiful Edwardian gardens landscaped by Thomas Mawson, we have one of the most enviable locations in the Lake District.

Built in 1910, many of Cragwood's original features have been retained and lovingly restored and includes beautiful wood panelling and magnificent fireplaces. Cragwood attracts guests from all over the world to experience our top quality food, drink and accommodation. With 23 bedrooms we are big enough to feel grand, but small enough to be intimate and relaxed.

Dining at Cragwood is an experience not to be missed. Under the direction of creative head chef Calvin Harrison, our team use only the finest local and seasonal ingredients. You'll discover a menu of imaginative and freshly prepared food.

We believe in celebrating the region we live in and embracing all that is special and unique about the area. Food heroes like the local farmer, fisherman and butcher are the key to our homegrown and local philosophy. Our chefs make everything fresh on the premises, we even have our very own resident chocolatier, pâtissier and speciality cake maker.

Relish Restaurant Rewards
See page 003 for details.

A regular on Trip Advisor's Certificate of Excellence listings, at Cragwood we pride ourselves on providing exceptional food and outstanding service from our fabulous location on the shores of Lake Windermere.

GOAT'S CHEESE THREE WAYS (SNOW, BEIGNET, MOUSSE), ROAST BEETROOT, BLACK OLIVE WHEEL & TRUFFLE DRESSING

SERVES 4

🍷 *Chenin Blanc Barrel Ferment, Jordan Vineyards, Stellenbosch (South Africa)*

Ingredients

Olive Tapenade
3 tbsp capers
6 anchovy fillets
250g black olives
small bunch parsley
salt and pepper
2-4 tbsp olive oil, 1 clove garlic

Black Olive Wheel
50g puff pastry, 200g olive tapenade

Goat's Cheese Snow
1 litre water
500ml lemon juice
500g goat's cheese
2 gelatine leaves (soaked in cold water)

Goat's Cheese Mousse
500g goat's cheese log
50ml full-fat milk
2 gelatine leaves (soaked in cold water)
100ml double cream

Goat's Cheese Beignet
250ml water
50g butter
70g plain flour
100g goat's cheese (grated)
4 eggs
½ tsp English mustard
salt and pepper
polenta (for dusting)
vegetable oil (for frying)

Beetroot
2 of each beetroot (candy, golden red)

Truffle Dressing
100ml aged balsamic, 100ml truffle oil

Method

For The Tapenade And Olive Wheel (Prepare ahead)
Pulse all the tapenade ingredients together, adding enough olive oil to form a paste. Roll out the puff pastry as thinly as possible. Spread the tapenade mix onto the puff pastry, roll into a cigar shape and freeze. Cut thin slices and bake at 180°C for about 8 minutes, or until golden brown.

For The Goat's Cheese Snow
Bring the water and lemon juice to the boil in a pan. Add the goat's cheese and gelatine. Blitz in a blender and pass through a fine sieve. Season with salt and pepper then chill. Churn in an ice cream machine until it reaches a 'snow' consistency.

For The Goat's Cheese Mousse
Roughly break up the gelatine, place in a food processor and blend until smooth. Warm the milk in a small bowl and add the gelatine to dissolve. Add this mix to the blender with the goat's cheese and blend until an even smoother consistency is achieved. Slowly add the double cream and blend until fully combined. Chill in the fridge until needed - at least 2 hours.

For The Goat's Cheese Beignet
Bring the water and butter to a simmer, then remove from the heat and add the flour. Cook slowly for about 8 minutes until the mixture leaves the side of the pan. Remove mixture from the heat and stir in the grated goat's cheese. Separate 3 of the eggs, adding 3 yolks and 1 whole egg to the mix along with the mustard, salt and a generous amount of pepper. Leave until cool, roll into small balls then dust in the polenta. Deep fry at 180°C for 3-4 minutes.

For The Roast Beetroot
Preheat the oven to 180°C. Place the unpeeled beetroot on a foil lined tray. Season and bake for an hour, or until soft. Peel when cool enough to handle. Cut into your desired shape. Serve warm.

For The Truffle Dressing
Mix all ingredients together until the liquid is fully combined.

To Serve
Serve as pictured.

> **Chef's Tip**
> Put all the ingredients on the plate before the goat's cheese 'Snow'. Taste. Taste. Taste.

LUNE VALLEY RACK OF LAMB, HERB CRUST, SWEET POTATO & RICH PORT JUS

SERVES 4

 Bourgogne Pinot Noir, Louis Latour, Burgundy (France)
Light and fruity red Burgundy from the excellent Louis Latour. Plenty of Pinot Noir bouquet and a smooth well rounded finish.

Ingredients

Meat

4 x 3 bone rack of lamb
mustard (to brush)

Herb Crust

4 slices stale bread
sprig flat parsley
4 sprigs thyme
4 sprigs coriander
4 sprigs rosemary
100g unsalted butter
1 tsp Dijon or English mustard

Fondant

2 sweet potatoes
150g butter
1 clove garlic
1 sprig thyme
75ml chicken stock

Purée

1.3kg sweet potatoes (pricked with a fork)
½ tsp salt and freshly ground pepper to taste
240ml buttermilk
240ml whole milk
6 tsp butter

Port Jus

450ml chicken or lamb stock
150ml ruby port
3 tbsp redcurrant jelly
150g *mirepoix* (carrots, onions, leeks)

To Serve

spring vegetables

5cm round cutter

Method

For The Herb Crust

Place all ingredients in a blender, blitz until green in colour.

For The Meat

Preheat oven to 200ºC.

Place the lamb in a pan to seal the meat until coloured. Transfer to the oven and cook for 5-7 minutes. Brush with mustard, cover with the herb crust and return to the oven for 2-3 minutes. Rest.

> **Chef's Tip**
>
> When the lamb rack is cooked, rest the meat for 8 minutes, then serve.

For The Fondant

Cut the potatoes with a 5cm round cutter, removing any sharp edges with a peeler. Place the flat side down on a griddle to mark, then place in a small pan with the rest of the ingredients. Cook for 10-12 minutes until tender.

For The Purée

Preheat oven to 220ºC.

Place the potatoes on a foil lined tray and bake for 45-60 minutes until tender. Peel when cool. Put the potato in a blender with rest of ingredients and blitz until smooth. Season to taste. Pass through a sieve and serve.

For The Jus

Put the *mirepoix* in a pan and sweat for 3-4 minutes. Add the port and redcurrant jelly, then the stock. Reduce to a syrup consistency.

To Assemble The Dish

Assemble as in the picture or as desired. Serve with spring vegetables.

MANGO SEMIFREDDO

SERVES 4

*Château Rieussec, 1er Cru Sauternes, Bordeaux
(France)
A classic sweet wine. Sauternes has great balance
of honeyed fruit, a superb rich flavour and a deep
long complex aftertaste.*

Method

To Prepare Your Moulds

Fold a small sheet of cling film into 3 and carefully wrap one
end of the mould. Make sure it is sealed so no mixture will seep
out during freezing. Set aside the moulds in the freezer for later.

For The Pâte à Bombe

Start by making the base for your semifreddo. Add the sugar
and water to a pan and boil until 121°C is reached.

For The Semifreddo (Allow time to freeze)

Whisk the egg yolks at high speed in a mixing bowl. When the
pâte à bombe has reached the desired temperature, slowly
whisk into the yolks until all has been incorporated, then whisk
at a high speed until cooled.

Lightly whisk the cream, then fold in the *pâte à bombe* mixture.
Add the mango purée and vanilla seeds. Pipe the mixture into
your prepared moulds and freeze until set.

To Serve

Decorate with raspberries, raspberry coulis and a spun sugar
shard (optional) Enjoy!

Chef's Tip

Always measure all ingredients properly and follow
instructions. Use a hot knife to get the semifreddo from
the mould.

Ingredients

Pâte à Bombe

300g caster sugar
200ml water

Semifreddo

10 egg yolks
750g mango purée
400ml double cream
1 vanilla pod (scraped)

Garnish (Optional)

raspberries
raspberry coulis
spun sugar shard

4 x 6½cm moulds

086
THE DUKE OF YORK

Brow Top, Grindleton, Near Clitheroe, Lancashire, BB7 4QR

01200 441 266
www.dukeofyorkgrindleton.com

Following a thorough but sympathetic refurbishment of the kitchen, bar and dining room in late 2007, Michael Heathcote has firmly established The Duke of York as one of the Ribble Valley's leading pub/restaurants, attracting scores of guests from far and wide who are keen to sample the restaurant which is commonly known amongst regulars as 'Lancashire's best-kept culinary secret.' The Duke of York serves classic British food with a modern and unique twist, showcasing not only the great skill of the kitchen team, but also their sense of humour.

Menus can change twice daily as Michael, alongside our talented kitchen team, make the most of the amazing local produce the Ribble Valley has to offer. Dishes aren't overly complicated, which allows the fantastic, seasonal produce to shine through. With a crackling log fire, a warm welcome awaits guests during the colder months, whilst in the summer a beautiful garden area offers al fresco dining.

Michael Heathcote is a proud Lancastrian, born and raised in Pleasington, and his passion for food stems from an early age when he helped his grandparents bake biscuits for their business in Blackburn. Michael trained in several establishments across England and Wales before setting off to gain experience in top restaurants in Australia, Canada and the USA.

On his return, he became head chef at Borrowdale Gates Country House Hotel in Cumbria, leading the kitchen for 8 years and achieving 2 AA Rosettes and entries in the Good Food Guide every year, before returning to the Ribble Valley to open the Duke of York.

Relish Restaurant Rewards
See page 003 for details.

In April 2014, The Duke of York was joined by
The Higher Buck in the beautiful village of
Waddington. Michael's second venture offers a
fantastic bar, a modern twist on pub classics
and seven beautifully appointed en-suite letting
bedrooms - www.higherbuck.com.

TWICE BAKED LANCASHIRE CHEESE SOUFFLE

SERVES 8

 Pinot Blanc, Domaine Sipp Mack
(Alsace, France)

Ingredients

Béchamel Sauce

50g butter
1 onion (finely diced)
50g plain flour
500ml full-fat milk

Soufflé

6 tbsp béchamel sauce
6 tbsp tasty Lancashire cheese (grated)
6 eggs (separated)

Topping

3 tbsp cream (seasoned with ¼ nutmeg, grated)
1 tbsp tasty Lancashire cheese (grated)

8 moulds or ramekin dishes

Method

For The Béchamel Sauce (Prepare ahead)

Melt the butter over a low heat and *sauté* the onions until soft, but not coloured. Add the flour and mix in completely to form a roux. Cook the flour through for a few minutes. Gradually whisk in small amounts of milk to the *roux*, whisking well between additions to remove any lumps and until the milk has been fully incorporated. Simmer over a low heat for a few minutes, stirring frequently to stop it catching on the bottom. Set aside until needed.

For The Soufflé (Prepare ahead)

Preheat the oven to 180°C (fan).

Line the moulds with softened butter, then dust with flour.

Gently warm the béchamel sauce and add in the cheese until it melts. Do not allow the mixture to overheat. Add the egg yolks and stir in well.

In a separate bowl, whip the egg whites to soft peaks, then gently fold into the cheese mixture. Fill the moulds to just below the top.

Place the soufflés into a large ovenproof dish. Fill the dish ¾ of the way up the sides of the moulds with water to make a *bain marie*. Bake for approximately 8 minutes until just set. Remove the moulds from the *bain marie* and allow to cool.

To Serve

Preheat the oven to 180°C (fan).

Remove the soufflés from the moulds and place onto an oven tray or into an ovenproof pan. Top with the seasoned cream and a scattering of grated cheese and bake for approximately 12 minutes until golden brown. Serve immediately from the oven with a beetroot and apple salad.

ROASTED RUMP OF LAMB, SPRING VEGETABLES, JERSEY ROYALS

SERVES 4

 Pinot Noir Reserve Especial, Sol de Andes, Casablanca (Chile)

Ingredients

Roasted Rump Of Lamb

2 sprigs rosemary
1 bulb garlic (cloves peeled)

Lamb Sauce

1kg lamb bones
red wine (glass of)
sherry vinegar (splash of)
1 litre water (approximately - to cover)
1 sprig rosemary

Spring Vegetables

500g broad beans (shelled, peeled)
200g baby carrots
4 baby fennel
bunch asparagus
200g spinach
Tenderstem broccoli
girolle mushrooms
tomatoes or beetroot (optional)
emulsified butter (to coat)

To Serve

Jersey Royals

Method

For The Lamb Sauce (Allow at least 4 hours)

Preheat the oven to 170°C (fan).

Roast the lamb bones for 2 hours until brown. *Deglaze* the oven tray with the red wine, then add the vinegar. Cover the bones with water and simmer gently for at least 2 hours to create a lamb stock. Pass through a fine sieve, then reduce to a sauce consistency. Season to taste with rosemary - no salt will be required.

Roasted Rump Of Lamb

Preheat the oven to 180°C (fan).

Trim the lamb of any excess fat and spike with the rosemary and garlic. Seal the lamb in a hot ovenproof pan, then roast in the oven for 8-10 minutes until pink. Leave to rest.

Spring Vegetables

Blanch the vegetables separately, excluding the spinach, in boiling, salted water until tender. Refresh in iced water. When ready to serve, reheat in *emulsified* butter and season.

To Serve

Carve the lamb and arrange as pictured. Serve with buttered Jersey Royal potatoes.

PAVE OF CHOCOLATE, HONEYCOMB

SERVES 18 (Freezes well)

Straw Wine, Rustenberg Estate, Stellenbosch,
(South Africa)

Ingredients

White Chocolate Base

175g white chocolate callets
175g feuillantine biscuits (crushed)

Chocolate Mousse

450g dark chocolate callets
150g egg yolk (7-8 egg yolks)
250g caster sugar
180ml fresh orange juice
600ml whipping cream

Chocolate Ganache

200ml whipping cream
225g dark chocolate callets

Honeycomb

160g caster sugar
40g golden syrup
180g liquid glucose
40ml water
24g bicarbonate of soda

To Serve

salted caramel ice cream

35x25cm baking tray (for the base, lined with
4 layers of cling film)
35x25cm baking tray (for the honeycomb,
lined with parchment)

Method

For The White Chocolate Base

Melt the chocolate over a *bain marie* and mix with the biscuits. Once mixed thoroughly, line the prepared tray evenly with the mixture.

For The Chocolate Mousse

Melt the chocolate over a *bain marie*. Set aside.

Add the yolks, sugar and orange juice into a bowl over a *bain marie* and whisk until a thick *sabayon* has formed. Pour in the dark chocolate and fold in carefully. Transfer to the fridge for half an hour to cool slightly. Once cooled, whip the cream to soft peaks. Fold into the chocolate mixture, then pour an even layer over the biscuit base. Leave to chill for approximately 1 hour in the fridge.

For The Chocolate Ganache

Bring the cream to the boil, then pour it over the chocolate callets. Mix until it has completely melted.

Float an even layer on top of the chocolate mousse. Leave to set in the fridge for an hour.

For The Honeycomb

Heat the sugar, golden syrup, glucose and water in a heavy bottomed pan until the sugar is fully dissolved. Heat the mixture to 148°C. Remove from the heat and add the bicarbonate of soda until fully incorporated. Allow to foam up, then pour onto a tray lined with baking parchment. When cool, break into pieces and store in an airtight container.

To Serve

Serve as pictured with salted caramel ice cream.

096
EVUNA

277-279 Deansgate, Manchester, M3 4EW
79 Thomas Street, Manchester, M4 1LQ

0161 833 1130
www.evuna.com Twitter: @EvunaManchester Facebook: www.facebook.com/evuna

Evuna originated in 2002 as a fine wine house with a main interest in importing fine Spanish wines from boutique wineries. In November 2003 Evuna Deansgate was born with one vision: to bring the people of Manchester the many hidden gems of the amazing diverse country that is Spain. To complement our amazing wines we brought the best chefs from Madrid to rustle up an eclectic mix of Spanish dishes.

Our main restaurant, situated on Manchester's most prestigious street Deansgate, aims to offer you the finest in Spanish food and drink, with food ranging from tapas to a la carte originating from the central regions in Spain.

Our signature dish is sea bass baked in rock salt, which is fabulously filleted at the table, and all our produce is cooked fresh daily on the premises.

Our northern quarter branch is the new kid on the block in this bustling, vibrant area of Manchester. The only tapas bar in the area, we bring you an authentic fresh tapas menu and Alhambra, Spain's premium draft beer from what is regarded as the leading craft brewery in Spain. To make a reservation at NQ, please call 0161 833 1130, or email nq@evuna.com.

Evuna's team is family through and through. Mother Frances, and husband and wife team Jane and Bosun have over a decade of restaurant experience with a passion for all things Spanish.

Our head chefs are Elena Ramos, who is passionate about fish and seafood, and Arkadiusz, a chef with many years' experience in fine dining, trained by German award-winning chef, Eyck Zimmer and American 2 Michelin star chef, Ryan Murphy

Leading front of house at Deansgate is Ewa Kralinska who has helped develop the business, and who specialises in wines and organising events. Natalia Samsoniuk (at NQ) helped to open Evuna in NQ. Natalia has a fine dining background, with many years of experience and a real passion for wines.

Relish Restaurant Rewards
See page 003 for details.

At both Evuna locations we offer a wine merchant service where customers can take their favourite wines home with them by the bottle or by the case, along with monthly wine tastings. In our small shop area you can browse our offers whilst enjoying a glass of wine and some tapas.

CALAMARES RELLENOS CON SALSA MARINERA
STUFFED SQUID WITH MARINERA SAUCE

SERVES 4

🍷 *Viña Toén, Monterrei Grape, Godello and Treixadura (Spain)*

Ingredients

Squid

4 medium squid (no larger than 30cm)
4 tbsp olive oil
1 large Spanish onion (finely diced)
½ red pepper (finely diced, optional)
1 fresh bay leaf (or use dried)
1 clove garlic (finely chopped or crushed)
salt and pepper
½ large bunch flat leaf parsley (finely chopped)
100ml Fino sherry (or dry white wine)
1 egg (hard boiled, finely chopped)

Marinera Sauce

leftover squid
60g margarine
1 small onion (chopped)
6 cloves garlic (*macerated*)
2 ripe tomatoes (chopped)
1 red pepper (diced)
1 tsp peppercorns (slightly crushed)
240ml water
salt and pepper
1 tbsp red wine vinegar

Garnish

lemon wedges
olive oil (to drizzle)

Method

For The Squid

Thoroughly clean the squid and separate the tentacles and wings from the body. Finely chop the squid wings and tentacles. You may leave the tentacles whole and cook them on the side.

Gently fry the onions and diced pepper (if using) in the olive oil for about 15 minutes until soft and the onion is starting to turn brown. Add the bay leaf, garlic and chopped squid and cook for about 3 minutes. Add the seasoning, the fino sherry and half the parsley. Cook for a further couple of minutes until the wine has almost evaporated, then remove from the heat. Remove the bay leaf and stir in the chopped egg and most of the remaining parsley. Check the seasoning and adjust if necessary.

Use this mixture to stuff the squid, securing with a cocktail stick to keep the filling in. Save any leftover squid for the sauce.

For The Marinera Sauce

Melt the margarine in a hot pan and fry the onion and garlic for about 2 minutes until softened, but don't allow them to brown. Add the tomatoes, leftover squid, peppers and water. Stir gently for about 2 minutes. Season to taste. Cover the pan and leave over a low heat for 5 minutes to allow the flavours to develop. Add the vinegar, return the lid to the pan and leave the sauce to boil for 5 minutes. Taste the sauce and season to your liking.

To Serve

When you are ready to eat, heat a griddle pan until it is smoking hot. Cook the squid for about 5 minutes, turning to ensure that it is charred all over.

Place your squid on the plates and spoon over a little of the sauce. Drizzle with olive oil and garnish with a piece of lemon. Sprinkle the remaining parsley over the top.

CARRILLADA DE CERDO IBÉRICO PORK CHEEK, ROASTED POTATOES & RED WINE JUS

SERVES 4

Finca Loranque Syrah and Tempranillo Blend,
La Mancha (Spain)
14 months of oak barrel ageing

Ingredients

Pork Cheeks

8 Ibérico pork cheeks
2 Spanish onions (peeled, thickly sliced)
2 sticks cinnamon
50g Demerara sugar
salt (to taste)
red wine (to cover)

Roasted Potatoes

2 large red potatoes
3 sprigs rosemary (chopped)
3 cloves garlic (chopped)
olive oil (to drizzle)
salt and pepper

Red Wine Jus

leftover cooking liquor from pork cheeks
same quantity of red wine
50g Demerara sugar

Roasted Vegetables

1 courgette (sliced)
1 aubergine (sliced)
1 red pepper (sliced)
salt and pepper
dried chilli flakes (pinch of)
olive oil (splash of)

Method

For The Pork Cheeks

Place the pork cheeks, onions, cinnamon, Demerara sugar and salt into a roasting tray, then pour over enough red wine to cover all the ingredients.

Cover the roasting tray with tin foil and transfer to the oven for 4 hours. Remove the pork cheeks and keep them warm. Strain the cooking juices through a fine sieve. Reserve for use in the red wine *jus*.

For The Potatoes

Preheat the oven to 180°C.

Cut the potatoes into 1½-2cm thick slices. Place into a roasting tray and drizzle with olive oil. Add the rosemary, garlic and seasoning. Combine thoroughly until all the potatoes have a covering of oil. Place the tray into the oven and roast the potatoes for 35-40 minutes until tender on the inside and golden brown on the outside.

For The Red Wine Jus

Pour the leftover cooking liquor from the pork cheeks into a large saucepan. Add the same amount of red wine and stir in the sugar. Bring to the boil, then reduce the liquid by three quarters over a medium heat. Add seasoning to taste.

For The Roasted Vegetables

Preheat the oven to 180°C.

Sprinkle the slices of courgette, aubergine and red peppers with salt, pepper, chilli flakes and olive oil and roast in the oven for 15 minutes.

To Serve

Serve as pictured.

CREMA CATALANA

SERVES 4

Moscatel (Spain)
A naturally sweet wine from the Navarra region

Method

To Make The Crema Catalana (Prepare at least 4 hours ahead)

Place the milk into a pan with the cinnamon and citrus zest and bring to the boil.

Mix the eggs, cornflour and sugar together in a large mixing bowl.

Once the milk has boiled and the flavours have infused, pass the milk through a sieve and add to the bowl with the rest of the ingredients. Whisk it together until you have a smooth paste.

Return the mixture to a clean pan and bring slowly to the boil, whisking thoroughly.

Pour the mix into the serving dishes and leave to set in the fridge until solid, for about 4 hours.

To Serve

Sprinkle the set desserts with white sugar so that the tops are completely covered. Using a blow torch, caramelise the sugar until it is golden brown. Alternatively, place under a hot grill to caramelise the sugar but don't leave it unattended as the sugar caramelises very quickly.

Ingredients

800ml full-fat milk
1 stick cinnamon
1 orange (zest of)
1 lemon (zest of)
4 egg yolks
60g cornflour
185g white sugar

To Serve

sugar (sprinkling of)

4 x 13½cm wide x 3cm deep crema Catalan dish

106
FONSECA'S
& DELIFONSECA
DOCKSIDE

Fonseca's: 12 Stanley Street, Liverpool, L1 6AF
Delifonseca Dockside: Brunswick Quay, Liverpool, L3 4BN

0151 255 0808
www.delifonseca.co.uk Twitter: #delifonseca

Delifonseca began life in 2006 on Stanley Street, created by passionate foodie Candice Fonseca. Keen to create a city centre modern delicatessen with old-fashioned service and quality values, it was opened with a casual dining room on the mezzanine level. Teaming up with local legend Martin Cooper (of Armadillo fame) the rest, as they say, is history. The restaurant revolved around a large blackboard menu which allowed truly seasonal cooking, the ability to showcase quality artisan deli produce and an ever changing menu to keep regulars happy. The menu evaded categorisation but 'global peasant' and 'bistro' were bandied about often using slow cooking methods.

In 2010 its bigger sister restaurant opened down at Brunswick Dock providing a larger food hall with butchery concession, more covers and parking.

Since then, both restaurants have gone from strength to strength evolving and changing. Both still operate a main course blackboard, but the chefs have been stretching their creative muscles and modern techniques are dotted throughout their menu boards. Stanley Street has been remodelled into a more glamorous space with a vintage chic wine bar in the former deli retail space and renamed Fonseca's to avoid confusion.

However, the essential ethos of Delifonseca remains the same; an obsession with good food with known provenance. A foodie haven, Delifonseca celebrates all things eating related, supplying and producing food that has been lovingly grown, produced or made and tastes all the better for it.

Relish Restaurant Rewards
See page 003 for details.

☺ HERBY FISHCAKES w/ CHUNKY CHIPS, DRESSED LEAVES, & A TOMATO CHUTNEY £10·95

⋈ FILLET OF HAKE TOPPED w/ AN ANCHOVY & SUNBLUSHED TOMATO TAPENADE. SERVED w/ CHUNKY CHIPS & DRESSED LEAVES. £13·95

⋈ FILLET OF SALMON w/ A CREAMY HERB & SUMMER VEGETABLE SAUCE SERVED WITH SAFFRON & LEMON POTATOES £14·95

✳ BLACK OLIVE GNOCCI w/ BASIL & COURGETTE PUREE, ROASTED BUTTERNUT SQUASH, BROAD BEANS, TOASTED PINE NUTS, BLACK OLIVE CRUMB £14·95

✳ ASPARAGUS & PEA RISOTTO, SERVED w/ GRIDDLED HALLOUMI AND ZUCCHINI £12·95

SOUS-VIDE w/ SOY SAUCE, GIN... SESAME. SERVED w/ STIR FRY

✳ LEMON + HERB BEEF & L... MEATBALLS SERVED IN A SPIC... ARRABIATA SAUCE w/ HERBY PEASHOOTS + PARMESAN SHAVI...

✳ HERDWICK LAMB RUMP (SO... SERVED w/ POMMES BOULANG... MINT PUREE, SEASONAL GREENS... JUS

✳ GUINEA FOWL STUFFED w/... + TRUFFLE CHICKEN MOUSSE. S... FONDANT POTATO, ROASTED CHER... TOMATOES, GREEN BEANS AN... MUSHROOM, WHITE WINE & CR...

✳ FILÉ GUMBO – TRADITIONAL LC... SPICY STEW OF PORK, SMOKED SA... ITALIAN SAUSAGE, SHRIMP w/... SERVED w/ BASMATI RICE

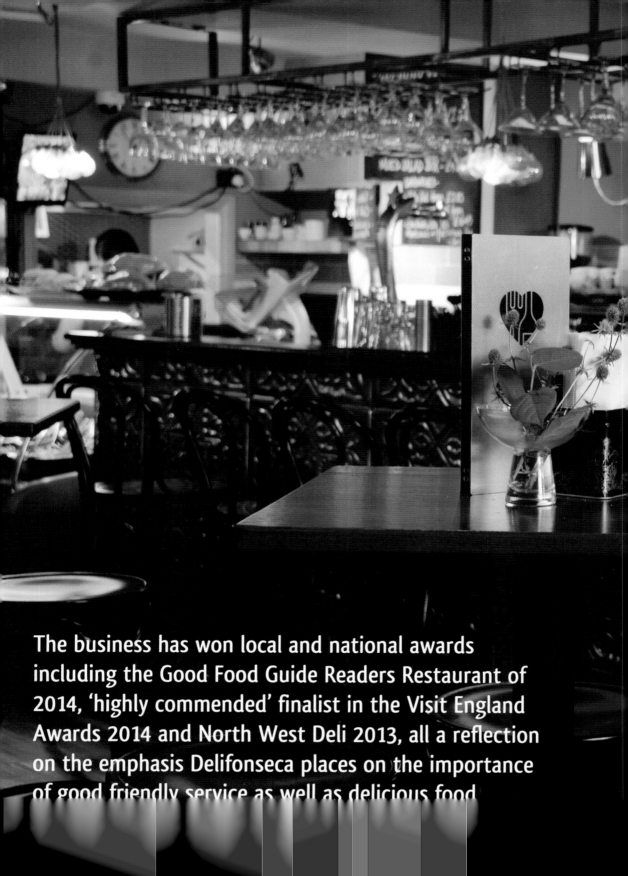

The business has won local and national awards including the Good Food Guide Readers Restaurant of 2014, 'highly commended' finalist in the Visit England Awards 2014 and North West Deli 2013, all a reflection on the emphasis Delifonseca places on the importance of good friendly service as well as delicious food.

KING PRAWNS WITH SAMPHIRE

SERVES 4

🍷 *Serra da Estrela Albariño, 2011*
(Spain)

Ingredients

24 raw king prawns (depending on size)
vegetable oil (for frying)
1 shallot (diced)
pepper (freshly ground)
fresh parsley (handful of, chopped)

Chilli Butter

250g butter
2 large red chillies
4 garlic cloves
salt (pinch of)

To Serve

500g samphire
crusty bread
1 lemon (cut into wedges)
fresh chilli or red pepper (finely diced)

Method

For The Chilli Butter

Cube the butter and then blitz, in a food processor, with the whole red chillies, garlic and pinch of salt. Roll into a 2cm wide log and wrap in cling film. Put in fridge to chill and set.

To Assemble The Dish

Heat a little vegetable oil in a large frying pan or wok on the stove. Add the king prawns and shallots.

Season with freshly ground pepper, colour on one side (approximately a minute), then turn over.

Add 100g of your chilli butter (diced) and the samphire. Fry for a further minute, stirring until the prawns are cooked.

Remove from the heat, throw in the chopped parsley and serve.

Decorate with finely diced red pepper (or fresh chilli if you really like a bit of a kick).

Garnish with a wedge of lemon and serve with crusty bread to mop up the lovely, buttery chilli juices.

Chef's Tip

This dish is a perfect light summer starter in July and August when English marsh samphire is in season. An ideal entertaining dish, it is quick and easy to prepare.

SMOKED DUCK BREAST WITH POMEGRANATE & CHICKPEA PILAF

SERVES 4

Fairvalley Pinotage, 2012 (South Africa)
or Carmen Gewürztraminer Reserva 2011 (Chile)

Ingredients

4 Cheshire Smokehouse duck breasts
(If you can't get hold of smoked, then pan fried
fresh duck breasts will be equally delicious)

Pickled Aubergine

2 aubergines (sliced lengthways)
olive oil (to brush)
1 stick cinnamon
3 star anise
1 tsp coriander seeds
1 tsp fennel seeds
2 tbsp pomegranate molasses
100ml vinegar and sugar reduction
(100ml vinegar and 100g caster sugar warmed
and reduced by half)

Chickpea Pilaff

300g tinned chickpeas
75g duck fat
½ large white onion (diced)
1 stick cinnamon
1 tsp smoked sweet paprika
½ head garlic (peeled, puréed)
300g basmati rice
1 litre reduced chicken stock
coriander (handful of, chopped)

Flatbread

100g plain flour
100g natural yoghurt
1 tbsp bicarbonate of soda

Garnish

walnuts (toasted)
pomegranate seeds
pomegranate molasses
garlic yoghurt
coriander leaves (ripped)
fresh parsley (chopped)

Method

For The Pickled Aubergine

Brush the aubergine slices with olive oil. Use a griddle to chargrill the aubergine and set aside to cool.

Prepare the pickle by combining all of the ingredients listed in a saucepan. Bring to a simmer, remove from the heat and let cool. Combine the aubergine with the pickle and refrigerate until required.

For The Chickpea Pilaf

Gently fry the onions, garlic and spices in the duck fat until the onions are translucent.

Add the rice. Coat in the duck fat and spice mixture.

Pour in the reduced chicken stock and simmer until the rice is cooked.

Add the chickpeas and some chopped coriander to add colour.

For The Flatbread

Combine the ingredients and mix until a dough is formed. Knead for a few minutes then shape into small, golf ball size pieces. Roll out into circles on a floured surface, brush with a little oil and chargrill for a couple of minutes on each side.

To Assemble

Slice the duck breasts (if you have trouble sourcing smoked duck breast then pan fried duck breasts work equally well). Place a warm flatbread in the centre of each plate. Add a large spoon of the warm chickpea pilaf. Top with a slice of pickled aubergine. Add fresh parsley and toasted walnuts. Place the sliced duck on top of the stack. Drizzle pomegranate molasses over the duck. Garnish with pomegranate seeds and ripped fresh coriander. Serve with garlic yoghurt either drizzled on top or on the side.

> **Chef's Tip**
>
> This dish takes inspiration for a middle eastern celebration dish 'fattee'. It's a great one for entertaining as it can all be prepped in advance and it becomes merely a feat of composition. The walnuts can be swapped for toasted pinenuts if you have a nut allergy guest.

WHITE CHOCOLATE & PISTACHIO MOUSSE WITH A RASPBERRY JELLY

SERVES 4

🍷 *Vidal Ice-wine 2010*
(Canada)

Ingredients

White Chocolate And Pistachio Mousse

200g digestive biscuits
100g butter (melted)
30g caster sugar
60g - approx 3 medium egg yolks
200ml full-fat milk
4 large leaves gelatine (22x7cm, soaked)
400g white chocolate (melted)
600ml double cream

Raspberry Jelly

250ml raspberry coulis
4 leaves gelatine (soaked for 10 minutes)

Garnish

50g pistachios (crushed)
raspberries and blackberries
mint leaves

25cm square tin (greased, lined)

Method

For The Chocolate And Pistachio Mousse

Blitz the digestive biscuits and add the melted butter.

Spread the biscuit mix into the tin and press firmly. Leave to set.

Whisk the egg yolks and sugar together in a bowl until pale. Heat the milk in a saucepan and bring to the boil. Slowly pour the milk onto the egg mixture whisking whilst pouring the milk, making sure the eggs do not scramble.

Once mixed together, add the gelatine, then stir in the melted chocolate. Pass the mixture through a sieve to remove any lumps. Leave to cool.

Whip the double cream and fold into the cooled egg and chocolate mixture. Pour onto the biscuit base and refrigerate for 4 hours to set.

For The Raspberry Jelly

Gently heat the coulis and stir in the soaked gelatine. Allow the coulis to cool, then pour over the top of the mousse. Leave to set in the fridge for 2 hours.

To Serve

Once the mousse and jelly have set, take the mousse out of the tin and cut into a size you prefer. Once cut, dust the sides of the mousse with the pistachio crumbs. This will give the mousse a lovely colour and extra crunch! Serve as pictured

Chef's Tip

This white chocolate mousse works well with all kinds of fruit. Don't be afraid to use other fruit coulis for your jelly depending on what's in season. Damson works wonderfully.

116
GEORGE & DRAGON

Clifton, Penrith, Cumbria, CA10 2ER

01768 865 381
www.georgeanddragonclifton.co.uk Twitter: @GeorgeDragonCli

The George and Dragon was transformed in 2008 when it was taken on by Charles Lowther. It has since built up an excellent reputation for its sustainable food philosophy, growing and rearing much of its own produce on the Lowther family estate.

The gardens at their nearby sister establishment, Askham Hall (gardens, café, restaurant and hotel www.askhamhall.co.uk), are home to a wide variety of fruit, vegetables, edible flowers, rare-breed pigs and goats, pedigree shorthorns and free-range chickens and ducks - all reared exclusively for the George and Dragon and Askham Hall.

It has won many accolades including a Taste of England silver award (Visit Britain 2012), Taste of Cumbria Awards in 2011 and 2013 and a Cumbria Life magazine food and drink award in 2014. With glowing reviews, the George and Dragon has a reputation for quality far and wide.

The food, extensive wine list and selection of local ales are not the only things to impress. The thoughtfully designed interior is something to be admired too, with beautiful, richly coloured rugs, bare-wooden tables, and intimate alcoves with photographs and archive prints from the family estate. With a relaxed atmosphere, along with the wonderfully friendly staff who make you feel so welcome, you won't want to leave. And you don't have to - 11 beautifully and individually designed bedrooms mean the George and Dragon is also perfect for a holiday in a quiet and secluded part of Cumbria.

Relish Restaurant Rewards
See page 003 for details.

The George and Dragon is not only well known for its excellent food but also for its philosophy and dedication to growing and rearing as much of its own produce as possible at nearby sister establishment Askham Hall (page 46), part of the family estate. Chef Ian Jackson and his kitchen team are dedicated and passionate about using the best quality, seasonal ingredients.

BRAISED SADDLEBACK PORK CHEEKS, PARSNIP PUREE, WARM MANGO & ROASTED CASHEW NUT SALAD

SERVES 4

 *Tomas Cusine Auzells (Spain)*

Ingredients

Pork Cheeks

8 pork cheeks (seasoned)
50ml vegetable oil
butter (knob of)
50g onion (diced)
50g carrot (diced)
50g leek (diced)
50g celery (diced)
2 tbsp tomato purée
200ml white wine
6 star anise

Parsnip Purée

2 parsnips (peeled, quartered, core removed)
30g unsalted butter
30ml double cream
salt and pepper

Mango And Roasted Cashew Nut Salad

30g caster sugar
30g unsalted butter
100g cashew nuts
1 mango (diced into 1cm chunks)

To Finish

dressed leaves

Method

For The Pork Cheeks

Brown the pork cheeks in a heated frying pan with a little oil and butter. Remove the cheeks and set aside. Using the same pan, brown the vegetables. Add the tomato purée and *deglaze* with wine. Place the pork cheeks and browned vegetables in a casserole dish, add the star anise and enough cold water to cover. Bring to the boil, then reduce to a very light simmer until tender - approximately 1½ hours. When the cheeks are tender, remove them from the cooking liquid. Strain the stock into another pan and reduce to a sauce consistency.

For The Parsnip Purée

Chop the parsnips into 2cm pieces. Add them to a pan, cover with cold water and add the butter. Bring to the boil, simmer until the liquid has evaporated and the parsnips are tender. Blend the parsnips and cream together to a soft velvety consistency. Season to taste.

Mango And Roasted Cashew Nut Salad

Heat the caster sugar in a frying pan until it makes a light caramel, then add the butter. When melted, add the cashew nuts and diced mango then caramelise. Once caramelised, set aside on a plate to cool.

To Serve

Smear parsnip purée onto the base of the plate and arrange 4 halves of the pig cheeks on the purée. Scatter the caramelised mango and cashew nuts onto the dish, drizzle the sauce over and around the whole dish. Finish with a little dressed leaf salad.

Chef's Tip

Preparation is the key to a successful end product.

PAN FRIED FILLET OF MONKFISH, HERB RISOTTO, CRISPY PARMA HAM, SWEET LEMON DRESSING

SERVES 4

🍷 *Pouilly Fuissé Bouchard Aîné & Fils (France)*

Ingredients

Monkfish

4 x 100g monkfish fillets (skinned, trimmed)
unsalted butter (knob of, cold, diced)
2 tbsp olive oil
salt and pepper
½ lemon (juice of)

For The Risotto

50g shallot (chopped)
1 clove garlic (crushed)
70g butter
200g carnaroli risotto rice
150ml white wine
1200ml vegetable stock (warm)
50g Parmesan cheese (grated)
20g chopped herbs (chives, dill, tarragon, chervil)
½ lemon (juice of)

Sweet Lemon Dressing

1 lemon (zest and juice of)
20g icing sugar
60ml light olive oil
salt and pepper (to season)

Courgettes

2 whole courgettes
olive oil (to brush)

Garnish

4 slices Parma ham

Method

To Make The Risotto

In a pan, sweat the shallots and garlic with 50g of the butter. Add the risotto rice and white wine. Reduce until the liquid has evaporated. Slowly, over 10-15 minutes, add most of the vegetable stock until the rice is *al dente*. Pour the rice onto a cold tray to stop it from cooking further.

For The Sweet Lemon Dressing

Mix the lemon zest, lemon juice, icing sugar and olive oil, season with salt and pepper and blend together.

For The Courgettes

Slice the courgettes diagonally, 5mm thick, season and brush with olive oil. Chargrill or lightly fry until golden on each side.

For The Parma Ham Garnish

Preheat the oven to 180°C.

Crisp the Parma ham by placing it between 2 sheets of greaseproof paper and 2 trays. Bake in the oven for 12 minutes.

To Cook The Monkfish

Preheat the oven to 180°C.

In an ovenproof frying pan, heat the olive oil and cold butter until golden brown. Season the monkfish fillets and add to the pan until 1 side is coloured, approximately 2 minutes. Turn the fish and place the pan in the oven to cook for a further 2-3 minutes. Remove from the oven, spritz the lemon over the monkfish then place it on a plate. Cover with tin foil and leave somewhere warm.

To Serve

Just before serving, heat the risotto rice, adding a little additional vegetable stock, grated Parmesan cheese, chopped herbs, remaining 20g of cold butter, lemon juice and salt and pepper.

Divide the rice and place in the centre of your 4 bowls. Slice each monkfish fillet into 3 pieces and place on the outside of the risotto. Arrange the courgettes on top of the rice and stand the Parma ham in the centre of the rice. Generously drizzle the sweet lemon dressing over and around the dish.

> **Chef's Tip**
> Seasoning is the key to all good food.

PEAR MILLE-FEUILLE WITH VANILLA CRÈME MOUSSELINE

SERVES 4

 *Royal Tokaji Late Harvest
(Hungary)*

Ingredients

Vanilla Crème Mousseline

300ml full-fat milk
½ vanilla pod
3 egg yolks
50g caster sugar
50g cornflour
10g plain flour
100ml double cream

Mille-Feuille

1 sheet ready rolled, all butter puff pastry
icing sugar (for dusting)

Pears

6 pears (peeled, halved, core removed)
150ml water
100g caster sugar
50ml white wine
½ vanilla pod

To Serve

icing sugar (to dust)
strawberries (poached and glazed)

Method

To Make The Crème Mousseline

In a pan, heat the milk with half a vanilla pod. In a separate dish, mix 3 egg yolks, the caster sugar, cornflour and flour together. Slowly add the heated milk to the egg mixture, mixing constantly, then return to the pan. Bring to the boil, whisking continuously for 3-4 minutes, then put in the fridge to cool. Whisk the double cream until it forms stiff peaks then mix it with 100g pastry cream to form a smooth texture. Add to a piping bag.

For The Mille-Feuille

Preheat the oven to 180°C.

Dust the puff pastry with a generous layer of icing sugar, sandwich between 2 baking sheets and bake for 10-15 minutes until crisp and golden brown. When cool, cut into 12 discs measuring 3x5cm.

For The Pears

Put the water, sugar, white wine and half a vanilla pod in a pan and bring to the boil to make a syrup. Place the pears in the pan with the syrup and cook until for 10-15 minutes until tender. Leave to cool in the syrup. Remove 4 halves of pear and blend with a little syrup to make the purée. Cube the remaining pears and set aside.

To Form The Dish

Take a plate or slate, design a pattern on it with the pear purée. Scatter a little diced pear, drizzle with the pear and vanilla syrup, then layer the puff pastry, piped mousseline, topping with diced pear, then repeat until you have 3 complete layers finishing with a puff pastry top. Place on the centre of the plate, decorate with the poached strawberries and dust with icing sugar. Simple but perfect.

Chef's Tip

Make sure the puff pastry is nicely caramelised with the icing sugar and the pastry cream is cooked long enough to lose the taste of flour.

126
HEATHCOTES BRASSERIE

23 Winckley Square, Preston, PR1 3JJ

01772 252 732
www.heathcotes.co.uk

eathcotes Brasserie opened in 1995 and has been a trailblazer for Preston and the North West's culinary dining scene for nearly two decades.

Chef Carl Noller has worked with Paul Heathcote for nearly half of that time, cooking innovative British and French classics around local producers.

The Brasserie's first menu featured Heathcote's famous black pudding, Goosnargh chicken and duck, first created by Paul and farmer Reg Johnson, Boddingtons ice cream, and the legendary bread and butter pudding with clotted cream and apricots.

Carl, and sous chef Jamie, continue to cook in the same style, but expect some more modern techniques; treacle cured salmon with whipped goat's cheese, sole with smoked broccoli and chocolate almond cake and raspberries with orange curd might sit along the classics.

There is also a weekly, seasonal changing, three course menu with a choice of lunch or dinner at £55 for two including a bottle of wine and mineral water. The main wine list consists of 60 wines chosen by Paul, every wine tasted by him. There is also a reserve list from the cellar.

Front of house is headed up by Paul Jordan and Luiza Woods, long term Heathcote team members, overseeing the smart, unpretentious casual service.

The dining room holds up to 90 covers and the balcony overlooks Paul's pizzeria and grill, The Olive Press. There is also a shabby chic cocktail bar for pre and after dinner drinks.

 Relish Restaurant Rewards
See page 003 for details.

25 years of Heathcotes food history is never ignored, but there are always new dishes, new ideas and new ingredients to work with. Good food needs good wine, not just mainstream but wines that sit alongside creative dishes.

TORBAY SOLE, SMOKED BROCCOLI PUREE, MORNAY BON BONS

SERVES 4

 Chablis Domaine Emile Petit 2011
(France)

Ingredients

4 fillets of sole
vegetable oil
salt and pepper

Mornay Bon Bons

45g butter
45g all-purpose flour
500ml milk
salt and pepper
nutmeg (pinch of)
80g Lancashire cheese (grated)
flour, beaten egg and Panko breadcrumbs
(to coat the bon bons)

Broccoli Purée

1 large broccoli head
15g butter
salt and pepper
smoked oil (to taste)

To Serve

Tenderstem broccoli (steamed)
micro leaves

Method

For The Mornay Bon Bons

Melt the butter in a pan. Add the flour and combine until the mixture is pale yellow in colour. Be careful not to overcook. Whisk in the milk and bring to the boil. Reduce the heat. Season with salt, pepper and nutmeg. Simmer for about 2-3 minutes, then stir in the cheese. Whisk thoroughly until it has melted. The sauce should have a thick consistency.

Allow to cool, then roll the mixture into small balls, about 2cm in diameter. Roll the balls in flour, dip into a beaten egg mixture, then roll in breadcrumbs.

For The Broccoli Purée

Bring a pan of salted water to the boil. Cut the broccoli into florets and chop the stalks into small pieces. Add these to the boiling water, then cook until tender. Plunge into iced water to chill.

Drain the broccoli in a colander and place in a Thermomix, or blender, along with the butter, salt and pepper and smoked oil.

For The Sole

Take a hot frying pan, add a little oil, season the sole with salt and pepper, then cook on one side until crispy and golden brown.

Turn over and cook for a further 30 seconds, then remove from the pan.

To Serve

Deep fry the bon bons (170°C) for 2-3 minutes until golden brown. Plate as pictured.

BRAISED PORK NECK, CARAMELISED APPLE, MINI ROAST POTATOES, RED & GREEN CABBAGE, CRUMBLED SCRATCHINGS

SERVES 4

Selbach Racy Riesling
(Germany)
The wine has a bright yet delicate apple fruit with good minerality and a crisp acidity. The finish is zesty with a hint of citrus.

Ingredients

1 pork neck fillet
salt and pepper

Pork Jus

3kg chicken bones
1kg pork bones
1 tbsp vegetable oil
150g onions (roughly chopped)
75g carrots (roughly chopped)
100g button mushrooms
2 cloves garlic (crushed)

Caramelised Apple

5ml olive oil
1 Bramley apple (peeled and turned into 8 pieces)
2 tbsp icing sugar (sieved)

Mini Roast Potatoes

2 large potatoes (peeled)
oil
butter (knob of)

Red And Green Cabbage

1 red cabbage, 1 Savoy cabbage
(outer leaves removed and both cut into 8 wedges)
butter (knob of)
salt and pepper

Crumbed Scratchings

1 sheet pig skin (cut into 1cm x 8cm slices)
salt

melon baller

Method

For The Pork Neck

Remove any sinew and roll the pork tightly in cling film. Place in a water bath at 62°C for 6 hours. Alternatively, braise in a roasting tray covered in tin foil at 150°C for 3¼ hours.

For the Pork Jus (Prepare ahead)

Preheat the oven to 200°C (fan).

Place the chicken bones and pork bones in separate roasting trays and cook in the oven for 1 hour, turning regularly to brown all over. Discard the fat from the trays and set the bones aside. *Deglaze* the trays by adding a small amount of water and scraping the bits from the bottom. Reserve the liquid.

Heat the oil in a pan and cook the onions until golden brown. Add the carrots, garlic and mushrooms and cook until the carrots are soft.

Add the chicken bones and the *deglazed* juice to the pan, then cover with water. Bring to a simmer, skimming the impurities that rise to the top. Simmer for 2 hours. Leave to cool.

Pass through a fine sieve or muslin sheet into a clean pan. Add the pork bones, place on a low heat and reduce by half. Pass through a sieve and continue to reduce until the mixture clings to the back of a spoon. Sieve again then chill.

For The Caramelised Apple

Caramelise the oil and icing sugar in a pan. Add the apple pieces and toss until richly coloured.

To Cook The Mini Roast Potatoes

Scoop out 3 balls per person from the potatoes using the melon baller. Boil in salted water for 5 minutes. Drain and allow to steam dry. Roast in the oil and butter until golden.

For The Red And Green Cabbage

Cook the 2 cabbages separately in boiling water for 5 minutes. Refresh in cold water. Before serving, bring back to the heat in water. Add butter and seasoning to finish.

For The Crumbled Scratchings

Preheat the oven to 180°C (fan).

Place the skin slices onto a baking tray covered with greaseproof paper. Sprinkle with a good pinch of salt, cover with greaseproof paper and press down with another tray. Transfer the trays to the oven for 20-25 minutes.

Crumble some of the cooked pieces over the pork and arrange a strip for decoration.

To Serve

Serve as pictured.

CHOCOLATE & ALMOND SAVARIN, ORANGE CURD & RASPBERRIES

SERVES 8

 Tokaji Aszu 5 Puttonyos
(Hungary)
One of the world's greatest sweet wines, full flavoured and luscious with hints of orange peel rising above the intense fresh fruit aromas.

Ingredients

Chocolate And Almond Savarin

1 medium orange
6 eggs
1 tsp baking powder
½ tsp bicarbonate of soda
250g caster sugar
50g cocoa
200g ground almonds

Orange Curd

6 Seville oranges (juice of, plus finely grated zest of 2 oranges)
2 eggs
100g caster sugar
110g unsalted butter
1 tsp cornflour

Tempered Chocolate Squares

200g dark bitter chocolate
100g couverture chocolate (broken into pieces)

Garnish

raspberries
icing sugar (to dust)
8 small sprigs of mint

8 x 8cm savarin moulds

Method

For The Chocolate And Almond Savarin

Place the whole unpeeled orange in a pan and cover with water. Bring to the boil and simmer for 2 hours until soft. Drain and when cool, cut into 4. You do not need to remove the pips.

Place the 4 pieces of cooked orange into a food processor. Add the eggs, baking powder, bicarbonate of soda, caster sugar, almonds and cocoa. Blitz to create a smooth paste.

Preheat the oven to 180°C (fan).

Pour the paste into the buttered and floured 8cm savarin moulds and bake for 15-20 minutes. Remove from the moulds and leave to cool.

For The Orange Curd

Place all the ingredients into a saucepan and dissolve together over a very low heat. Stir continuously with a wooden spoon until the curd coats the back of the spoon.

Allow to cool for 5-10 minutes.

For The Tempered Chocolate Squares

In a *bain marie,* heat up the dark bitter chocolate until it reaches 46°C degrees. Add the couverture chocolate and cool it down to around 28-20°C degrees until it reaches a paste-like consistency. Cling film a flat tray and spread as thinly as possible. Leave to cool, then cut into squares.

To Serve

Pour the cooled orange curd into the hole of each savarin. Top with a tempered chocolate square and fresh raspberries. Dust with icing sugar and garnish with a sprig of mint.

THE INN AT WHITEWELL

Forest of Bowland, Near Clitheroe, Lancashire, BB7 3AT

01200 448 222
www.innatwhitewell.com

Based in the beautiful Forest of Bowland, designated an area of outstanding natural beauty, the Inn sits high on the bank of the River Hodder and commands breathtaking views down the valley, taking in the fells to the moors above. The Inn at Whitewell is an increasingly rare entity, a traditional rural inn. This listed building, which dates back to the 1400s, is stuffed full of antiques and old sporting art. There are 23 bedrooms, all glamorous, some with gorgeous antique cabinet baths and others with real peat fires. Whether you come to fish for sea trout or salmon, walk the dogs, read the papers or sample the extensive wine stocked by the in-house vintners; wellies, high heels, dogs and children all meld together to create a unique and very relaxing atmosphere.

The Inn deservedly has a good reputation and many awards for its food. Head chef Jamie Cadman, now in his 16th year, runs a crew of 11, ably supported by his two sous chefs, Gemma and James, producing brilliant local food. His ethos is to use only the best of local ingredients, cooked simply, to let the real quality shine through. Seasonal grouse from Lancashire Moor, pheasant and partridge from Dunsop shoot, Bowland beef and Lonk lamb from Burholme Farm are staples on the menu, all easily seen from the Inn's windows.

Relish Restaurant Rewards
See page 003 for details.

We thought it appropriate to feature grouse due to the popularity of this wonderful game bird. We are lucky enough to get our birds direct from Lancashire Moor where Charles shoots; fortunately, the other guns are a far better shot than him.

HOME CURED SALMON, THAI CRAB CAKES, PICKLED VEGETABLES, WASABI CREAM

SERVES 4

 Fairhall Downs Pinot Gris 2011, Marlborough (New Zealand)

Ingredients

Home Cured Salmon

1 side salmon (scaled and pin boned - ask your fishmonger to do this for you)
250g course sea salt
200g soft brown sugar
100g root ginger
5 sticks lemon grass
1 red chilli
100g fresh coriander (chopped)

Crab Cakes

50g fresh white crab meat
50g dark crab meat
50g skinless salmon (blitzed)
25g skinless salmon (diced)
50g dry potato purée
1 tbsp green Thai paste
½ lime (juice of)

Pickled Vegetables

2 small carrots
1 small cucumber
100ml white wine vinegar
1 tsp salt
3 tbsp white sugar

Wasabi Cream

1 tbsp wasabi paste
100ml double cream

Garnish

1 lime (cut into 4 wedges)
parsley

Method

For The Home Cured Salmon (Start preparing 3 days ahead)

Blitz all the marinade ingredients, except the coriander, in a food processor. Spread over the flesh of the salmon, wrap tightly in cling film and leave on a tray in the fridge for 48 hours. Wash off the marinade, pat dry and cover with the chopped coriander, wrap again and leave in the fridge for 24 hours before using it.

To Make The Crab Cakes

Mix all ingredients together, taste and adjust the seasoning. More Thai paste can be added to suit your own preference. Split into 4 balls and flatten into patties.

For The Pickled Vegetables

Using a peeler, strip the vegetables and place into a stainless steel bowl. Add the sugar, salt and vinegar. Mix well and leave for at least an hour before serving.

For The Wasabi Cream

Blend the wasabi paste into the double cream.

To Serve

Pan fry each crab cake for about 3 minutes each side. Thinly slice the salmon and arrange on a plate along with the pickled vegetables. Drizzle the wasabi over the crab cake.

> **Chef's Tip**
> When slicing the salmon, use a thin bladed knife and wipe with some damp kitchen roll to stop the salmon sticking to the knife.

ROAST LOCAL GROUSE, ROAST ROOTS, SPICED PEARS, BREAD SAUCE

SERVES 4

 Mascarello Nebbiolo 2011, Langhe, Piedmont (Italy)

Ingredients

Grouse

2 brace young grouse (dressed)
4 rashers back bacon
red wine (dash of)
570ml chicken stock

Spiced Pears

2 pears (peeled)
2 strips lemon peel
1 star anise
½ cinnamon stick
4 allspice berries
2 cloves
1 blade mace
150ml dry white wine
100g granulated sugar

Roast Roots

2 parsnips (peeled, cut into 6cm batons)
2 carrots (peeled, cut into 6cm batons)
50g butter
drizzle of honey (small amount)

Bread Sauce

500ml milk
200g stale white farmhouse style bread
(crusts removed)
½ small onion (studded with 2 cloves)
2 bay leaves
salt

To Serve

potatoes

Method

For The Spiced Pears

Place all the ingredients, except the pears into a pan and bring to a simmer. Stand the pears in the pan. They should be covered just up to the stalk, add more water if needed. Cover with a lid and gently poach for approximately 30 minutes, or until tender. Allow to cool in the liquor. Dice when cool.

For The Roast Roots

Preheat the oven to 170ºC (fan).

Melt the butter in an ovenproof frying pan, add the roots and fry until they start to colour. Put the pan in the oven for 20 minutes, then drizzle over the honey and return the pan to the oven for a further 5 minutes. Keep warm until serving.

To Make The Bread Sauce

Bring the milk, onion and spices to a simmer, take off the heat and allow to infuse for 30 minutes. Remove the onion and spices then add the bread, stirring over a gentle heat until it has broken down to a smooth sauce with the consistency of thick cream. Cover with cling film to avoid a skin forming and keep warm.

For The Grouse And Jus

Preheat the oven to 170ºC (fan).

Season and seal the birds in a hot pan. Lay a rasher of bacon over each bird and cook in the oven for approximately 12 minutes, depending on how pink you like it.

Allow to rest for 15 minutes before carving.

Meanwhile, shred the bacon and put back into the pan, *deglaze* with a little red wine and add the chicken stock. Bring to the boil and reduce by about half.

> **Chef's Tip**
> Allow the birds to rest for at least 10 minutes before taking off the bone to avoid losing the natural juices.

To Serve

Place the boned grouse on a spoonful of bread sauce and arrange the diced pear into a little ramekin on the side. Pour over the roasting *jus*. Serve with roast root vegetables and potatoes.

MILLIONAIRE TORTE

SERVES 8

🍷 *Bacalhoa Moscatel de Setubal 2007
(Portugal)*

Ingredients

Base
150g shortbread
125g butter (melted)

Mousse
397g tin condensed milk (unopened)
125g butter
125g golden syrup
2½ leaves gelatine (softened in cold water)
250ml double cream (whipped)

Chocolate Jelly
45g caster sugar
225ml water
30g cocoa powder
3 leaves gelatine (softened in cold water)

To Serve
vanilla ice cream
chocolate sauce
mint (sprig of)

20cm round loose bottomed tin (lightly greased)

Method

To Make The Base
Blitz the shortbread in a food processor and add the melted butter. Press into your prepared tin.

To Make The Mousse (Prepare at least 3 hours before)
Start by turning the condensed milk into toffee. Place the unopened can of condensed milk into a large pan ensuring it is covered with boiling water. Gently simmer for 2-3 hours, topping up the water if necessary. Don't leave it unattended as it could explode if the water dries up. You can do a few of these at a time as they will keep, unopened, in your cupboard until the use by date.

Warm the toffee, butter and golden syrup in a *bain marie*, add the softened gelatine then pass through a sieve. Chill in the fridge for 10 minutes. Fold in the whipped cream, then pour the mousse over the shortbread base. Leave to set in the fridge until firm - approximately 2 hours.

For The Chocolate Jelly
Bring the sugar and water to the boil, add the cocoa powder and simmer for 5 minutes. Add the softened gelatine and pass through a sieve.

Set aside to cool, then pour on top of the toffee mousse. Chill and set in the fridge for 30 minutes.

To Serve
Serve as pictured with a *quenelle* of ice cream, chocolate sauce and a sprig of mint.

> **Chef's Tip**
> When slicing the torte, dip your knife in hot water to give a cleaner cut.

146
JAMES MARTIN MANCHESTER

Manchester235, 2 Watson Street, Manchester, M3 4LP

0161 828 0300
www.jamesmartinmanchester.co.uk Twitter: JamesMartinMCR

Located in Manchester235 Casino, James Martin Manchester has enjoyed incredible success in its first year, setting out its stall as an institution for modern, uncomplicated, flavoursome British cuisine.

Situated on a spacious mezzanine area away from the main gaming floor, the restaurant is headed up by head chef Doug Crampton, who has worked alongside James Martin for years, helping him to launch Leeds Kitchen as sous chef, before taking on the head chef role in Manchester.

Housed in the Great Northern Warehouse, the restaurant provides guests with an elegant yet rustic setting, having maintained the Victorian bricks and industrial chic steel girders, which complement luxury vintage-style fabrics and eclectic artwork.

The restaurant has also introduced diners to the 'Meat Market', a theatrical walk-in fridge which displays the different cuts of meat served up in the kitchen.

James and Doug have worked tirelessly to produce a menu which offers a mix of James Martin's classic British style of cuisine, big on flavour and uncontrived in its simplicity.

The front of house team is on hand to offer advice on selecting the ideal wine to complement the meal, with firm favourites including Thai crab risotto, British Wagyu beef and hot sticky toffee pudding.

Alongside the à la carte menu, there are a number of additional menus including the Sunday roast menu and pre theatre menu.

Relish Restaurant Rewards
See page 003 for details.

Pleasing on the palate. Simple yet effective. Phrases that resonate throughout the menu put together by James Martin and Doug Crampton. With an accompanying wine list set to tantalise the tastebuds, the most difficult thing is trying to choose what to order!

BRITISH WAGYU BEEF, SLOW COOKED EGG YOLK, RAPESEED & MUSTARD DRESSING

SERVES 4

 Merlot, Grand Chataigner, Vin de Pays d'Oc
(France)

Ingredients

Mustard Mayonnaise

2 medium egg yolks
25ml white wine vinegar
25g English mustard
200ml vegetable oil
100ml extra virgin rapeseed oil
3g table salt

Pickles

300ml water
200ml white wine vinegar
100g caster sugar
1g peppercorns
1 medium carrot (peeled)
1 banana shallot (peeled)

Wagyu Tartar

250g Wagyu fillet (finely diced)
25g shallots (finely diced)
25g gherkins (diced)
25g baby capers
Maldon sea salt
cracked black pepper

Rapeseed Oil Dressing

100ml extra virgin rapeseed oil
25ml sherry vinegar
25ml Worcestershire sauce
10ml Tabasco
3g salt

To Garnish

5 free range medium egg yolks
baby thyme
tempura capers berries

Method

For The Mustard Mayonnaise

Combine the egg yolks, vinegar, English mustard and salt in a bowl. Mix the 2 oils together and slowly pour into the egg yolk mixture whilst whisking, ensuring the oil is being *emulsified* into the mayonnaise. Once all the oil is added, check the seasoning and chill.

For The Pickles

Bring the water, vinegar, sugar and peppercorns to the boil, then chill. Thinly slice the shallots into ringlets. Square off the sides of the carrot before slicing on a *mandolin* into long strips. Place the vegetables in the pickling liquor and leave for 15 minutes.

For The Eggs

Place the whole eggs in a water bath for 1 hour at 62ºC.

For The Rapeseed Oil Dressing

Add the Worcestershire sauce, Tabasco, sherry vinegar and salt to a small bowl and *emulsify* the rapeseed oil into the mix.

To Plate Up

Combine the ingredients for the tartar together in a bowl. Season with the rapeseed oil dressing, sea salt, and black pepper. Remove the eggs from the water bath, crack open and carefully remove the white just to leave the yolk. Garnish the plate with the mustard mayonnaise, pickles, caper berries and baby thyme before finishing with a little more of the rapeseed oil dressing.

Chef's Tip

We use a specialist supplier to provide us with the Wagyu. If you can't get hold of any, use the best possible fillet available to you. If you don't have a water bath, a poached egg would be a good accompaniment as well.

BROWN BUTTER POACHED GIGHA HALIBUT, BABY FENNEL, PICKLED PEAR & JERSEY ROYALS

SERVES 4

 Torrontes, Andean Vineyards (Argentina)

Ingredients

Halibut

4 x 120g portions Gigha halibut
200g brown butter

Halibut Jus

1kg halibut bones
1 onion (sliced)
1 clove garlic (crushed)
200ml white wine
1 litre chicken stock
15g thyme
50g butter
lemon juice (squeeze of)

Pear And Brown Butter Purée

4 large pears
100g brown butter
5g Maldon sea salt

Seaweed Butter

50g butter (diced)
50g dried nori seaweed
10ml lemon juice

Saffron Pickled Pear

300ml water
200ml vinegar
100g caster sugar
saffron (pinch of)
1 pear (peeled)

To Serve

5 baby fennel (reserve tops for garnish)
150g samphire
250g Jersey Royal potatoes (cooked)

Method

For The Halibut Jus

Heavily roast the bones in a pan until golden. Once golden, add the onion and garlic, then caramelise. *Deglaze* the pan with the white wine and cook until reduced by half. Add the chicken stock and simmer for 20 minutes. Pass through muslin and a fine sieve into a pan, return to the heat and reduce by two thirds. Add the thyme and cook for a further 5 minutes on a low heat and then pass again. To finish, whisk the butter into the sauce and season with salt and lemon juice.

For The Pear And Brown Butter Purée

Peel and dice the pears, discarding the core, and add to the brown butter. Cook for 10 minutes on a low heat until soft. Blend to a smooth purée and pass through a fine sieve. Season with sea salt and keep warm.

For The Seaweed Butter

Blitz the nori seaweed to a fine powder and mix with the softened butter and lemon juice.

For The Saffron Pickled Pear

Combine the water, vinegar, sugar and saffron together and bring to the boil. Once boiled, leave to infuse for 15 minutes before chilling. Peel the pear and slice on a *mandolin* into thin discs. Dip the pear slices into the chilled pickle and leave for 30 seconds before removing.

To Assemble

Thinly slice the Jersey Royal potatoes and warm through in the seaweed butter. Individually vac pac the halibut with the brown butter and cook for 8 minutes at 60ºC. Whilst the halibut is cooking, char the baby fennel using a blow torch until soft and dark in colour. Add the samphire to the pan with the potatoes and cook for a further 1 minute. Place a spoonful of purée into a deep bowl, add the Jersey Royals and the samphire. Remove the fish from the vac pac bag and season with sea salt and lemon juice. Garnish with the charred baby fennel, pickled pear and fennel tops and finish with the halibut *jus* and a little seaweed butter.

Chef's Tip

If you don't want to poach the fish, you could pan fry until golden and serve the same way.

GLAZED CAMBRIDGE CREAM, APPLES & HAZELNUTS

SERVES 4

 Late Harvest Sauvignon Blanc, Errazuriz Estate (Chile)

Ingredients

For The Cambridge Cream
5 medium egg yolks
65g caster sugar
300ml double cream
1 vanilla pod
10g caster sugar (extra for glazing)

For The Apple Granite
2kg Bramley apples
200g caster sugar
25ml lemon juice
2 leaves gelatine (soaked in cold water)

For The Hazelnut Praline
200g caster sugar
50ml water
200g shelled hazelnuts (toasted)

For The Apple Purée
500g Bramley apples (peeled, diced)
100g caster sugar
¼ vanilla pod

For The Apple Crisps
100ml stock syrup
1 apple

To Serve
1 apple (diced)
4 x 4cmx10cm stainless steel rectangular moulds

Method

For The Cambridge Cream
Whisk the egg yolks and sugar until light and fluffy. In a separate pan, add the cream and vanilla and bring to the boil. Leave to infuse, off the heat, for 5 minutes. Add the vanilla infused cream to the egg yolk mixture and whisk until it is fully incorporated. Return back to the original pan and cook for 10 minutes on a low heat, stirring constantly until thickened, or it reaches 80°C. Remove from the heat, pour into the moulds and chill for 4 hours, or until set.

> **Chef's Tip**
>
> The cream can also be set in any shallow dish you have. Using a temperature probe whilst cooking your custard ensures you take it to the correct temperature in order for it to set and not overcook. All elements of this dish can be prepared in advance.

For The Apple Granite
Juice the apples, then warm a ¼ of the apple juice with the lemon and sugar. Add the soaked gelatine and ensure it dissolves fully. Add to the remaining juice and place into the freezer. Freeze for 3 hours, regularly breaking the ice with a whisk.

For The Hazelnut Praline
Combine the water and sugar and cook on a high heat until it caramelises. Add the toasted hazelnuts, stir, then remove from the pan onto parchment paper. Leave to cool. Once cool, blitz half to a fine crumb and break the remaining half with a rolling pin.

For The Apple Purée
Cook the apples with the sugar and vanilla until softened, then blitz to a smooth purée and pass through a fine sieve.

For The Apple Crisps
Thinly slice the apples on a *mandolin*, remove the core and dip into the stock syrup. Dehydrate for 6 hours at 70°C, or overnight in a low oven.

To Assemble
Sprinkle the sugar on top of the Cambridge cream and glaze using a blow torch until golden. Remove from the mould. Garnish the plate with the hazelnut crumb and the hazelnut praline. Add a spoonful of apple purée and diced fresh apple. Finally, add the apple granite and crisps.

156
THE LEATHES HEAD
COUNTRY HOUSE HOTEL & RESTAURANT

Borrowdale, Keswick, Cumbria, CA12 5UY

01768 777 247
www.leatheshead.co.uk Twitter: @LeathesHead Facebook: www.facebook.com/theleatheshead

The Leathes Head is a charming Edwardian country house hotel and restaurant, situated in the beautiful, unspoiled Borrowdale Valley in the Lake District. With stunning views and a welcoming atmosphere, guests can truly escape, relax and unwind in this hidden corner of Cumbria.

Dining at The Leathes Head is an integral part of any stay. The dining room commands impressive vistas out towards the pretty Derwentwater and the fells beyond.

Holder of one AA Rosette, the restaurant treats diners to a menu of locally grown and reared produce, including Herdwick lamb from Yew Tree Farm in Rosthwaite, local milk and free range eggs, fresh meat from Lakes Speciality Foods in Kendal and cheese from The Cheese Larder, as well as other Cumbrian producers.

The Leathes Head is passionate about its food and head chef, Daniel Hopkins, is abreast of all the latest culinary techniques. He is also keen on a centuries old skill of adding flavour through smoking.

The menu is brimming with fine dining options impeccably prepared using local ingredients and herbs sourced from the surrounding grounds and valley. These include heather for smoking the Herdwick lamb, rosemary for making parfait, lavender for rhubarb crumble, and wild garlic and chives seasoning picked on chef's regular foraging ventures in and around the hotel's two acres of grounds.

One of the star features of the menu at The Leathes Head is the locally sourced Herdwick lamb. This delicately flavoured award-winning meat is unique to the area and has a PDO status (Protected Status of Origin). It was even served to HM The Queen during her Coronation!

Relish Restaurant Rewards
See page 003 for details.

Relax, nurture your soul and invest in your wellbeing.

ENGLISH ASPARAGUS, BASIL OIL, QUAIL EGGS, BALSAMIC VINEGAR

SERVES 4

🍷 *Lofthouse Sauvignon Blanc, Marlborough (New Zealand)*

Ingredients

20 English asparagus spears
8 quail eggs
½ lemon (juice of)
salt (pinch of)
cracked black pepper

Garlic Vinaigrette

100ml olive oil
20ml white wine vinegar
1 clove garlic (crushed)
½ tsp Dijon mustard

Basil Oil

80g basil leaves
200ml good quality virgin rapeseed oil

500ml good quality Modena balsamic vinegar

Garnish

mixed baby salad leaves

Method

For The Garlic Vinaigrette

Whisk all the ingredients together to form the garlic vinaigrette.

For The Basil Oil

Blend the basil in a food processor, then add the oil until the mixture is well combined. Pour into a saucepan and gently bring to a temperature of 104°C, then pass through a fine *chinois* or muslin.

For The Balsamic Vinegar

Reduce the vinegar over a medium heat until a thick syrupy texture is achieved.

For The Quail Eggs

Poach the quail eggs in water with the lemon juice for 3 minutes.

> **Chef's Tip**
> Quail eggs are an excellent alternative and are cholesterol free. They are also delicious slowly fried in garlic butter.

To Serve

Blanch the asparagus in salted water for 1 minute, then remove. Use a pastry brush to brush the balsamic syrup across the plate. Arrange the asparagus in a neat pile on top of the syrup. Drizzle the vinaigrette on the asparagus. Garnish with mixed baby salad leaves. Place the quail eggs on top and finish with basil oil and cracked black pepper on the eggs. Serve immediately.

YEW TREE FARM HERDWICK HOGGET, BRAISED BREAST, RACK, HEATHER, BROAD BEANS, PANCETTA, PORT JUS

SERVES 4

🍷 *Viña Mar Reserva Especial Cabernet Sauvignon, (Chile)*

Ingredients

Hogget (lamb 12–18 months)

1 hogget breast
1 x 8 bone rack of hogget (French trim)
4 rashers pancetta
1 bunch heather
sea salt (sprinkling)
butter (knob of)

Port Jus

400ml port
600ml good quality lamb stock
Maldon sea salt (to taste)
honey (to taste)

Puy Lentils

200g puy lentils
1 stick celery (chopped)
1 carrot (chopped)
4 shallots (chopped)
2 cloves garlic (crushed)
50ml port
400ml lamb stock
oil (to *sauté*)
butter (knob of)

Broad Beans

200g broad beans (shelled)
butter (knob of)

Method

For The Breast (Allow 12 hours)

Remove any bones and skin from the breast, roll tightly and tie with butcher's string. Smoke in a stove top smoker for 8 minutes with the heather. Vacuum pack and cook *sous vide* for 12 hours at 68°C. Remove from vacuum pack and sear in a hot pan on the stove top until caramelised on all sides. Cut into 4 pieces and keep warm.

> **Chef's Tip**
> An alternative method to sous vide: After smoking, brown on all sides in a deep roasting tray, remove breast. In the same tray, fry some chopped onions, carrots and celery. Return the lamb breast to the tray, add stock to cover. Place baking parchment over the lamb, then cover the whole tray with foil. Cook for about 1½-2 hours on 160°C or until tender.

For The Puy Lentils

Sauté the chopped vegetables with the garlic until softened, then add the lentils. Fry for 2 minutes, *deglaze* with the port and reduce until absorbed by the lentils. Cover with the lamb stock and cook, covered, for 8 minutes on a medium heat or until the lentils are tender. Season to taste. Stir in a small cube of butter. Keep warm.

For The Rack

Preheat the oven to 220°C. Pan fry the rack on all sides until the fat is rendered and a good colour is achieved. Put the rack into the oven and cook for 5 minutes. Leave to rest in a warm place. Finish with sea salt and a knob of butter on top.

For The Port Jus

Reduce the port in a pan until syrupy in texture. Add the lamb stock and reduce by half. Season to taste with Maldon Sea Salt and honey.

For The Pancetta

Preheat the oven to 180°C. Lay the pancetta on a tray covered with greaseproof paper. Cover with more paper and a heavy tray. Bake in the oven for 12 minutes or until crisp.

For The Broad Beans

Warm through in a small amount of butter.

To Serve

Place the puy lentils in the centre of the plate. Arrange the breast next to the puy lentils. Lay the rack on the lentils, resting on the breast and arrange the buttered broad beans and pancetta around the lamb.

CHOCOLATE BAR, CARAMELISED WALNUT ICE CREAM, SALT CARAMEL

SERVES 8

San Emilio Pedro Ximenez Solera Reserva Emilio Lustau (Spain)

Ingredients

Chocolate Bar

100g plain chocolate
100g unsalted butter
2 eggs
100g caster sugar
50g plain flour
10g cocoa
2g baking powder

Caramelised Walnut Ice Cream

10 egg yolks
380g caster sugar
285ml full-fat milk
1 vanilla pod
200g walnut halves
1 tbsp groundnut oil
1 lemon (juice of)

Salt Caramel

175g light brown soft sugar
300ml double cream
50g butter
½ tsp Maldon sea salt

Garnish

18 chocolate filled raspberries
200g melted chocolate
edible flowers

8 rectangular moulds (8cmx4cm)

Method

To Make The Chocolate Bar

Preheat the oven to 180°C.

Melt the butter and chocolate in a *bain marie*. Whisk the eggs and sugar together until the mixture is light and airy. Mix the flour, cocoa and baking powder together in a large bowl. Carefully fold the melted chocolate into the whisked egg and sugar mixture, then fold this into the flour. Divide between 8 individual moulds and bake for 15 minutes.

For The Caramelised Walnut Ice Cream

Whisk together the egg yolks and 330g of the sugar. Bring the milk and vanilla pod to the boil, then add it to the sugar mixture. Return to the pan and cook slowly for about 10 minutes until it coats the back of a spoon. Allow to cool.

Toast the walnuts in a little oil in a pan over a medium heat. Add the remaining 50g of sugar and cook until the sugar turns to caramel. Carefully add the lemon juice then remove from the heat. Cool and chop finely. Add the walnuts to the cooled ice cream mixture. Churn in an ice cream machine.

To Make The Salt Caramel

Combine all the ingredients in a saucepan. Stir over a low heat until the sugar has dissolved. Turn up the heat and bubble for 2-3 minutes until golden and syrupy. Leave to cool for 30 minutes before serving.

To Serve

Brush melted chocolate across the plate. Using a small piping bag, fill the raspberries with chocolate then decorate the plate by drawing diagonal lines. Remove the chocolate bar from the mould and place in the centre of the plate. Arrange the raspberries next to the chocolate bar. Finish with a *quenelle* of the salt caramel at one side. Serve immediately, with a scoop of caramelised walnut ice cream surrounded by edible flowers in a separate bowl.

Chef's Tip

The recipe for the chocolate bar can be used in all sorts of moulds and with different variations. For example, you can layer biscuits or white chocolate inside the chocolate mix to create a favourite dessert.

166
LUNYA

18-20 College Lane, Liverpool One, Liverpool, L1 3DS

0151 706 9770
www.lunya.co.uk Twitter: @Lunya Facebook: www.facebook.com/Lunya

Set in the heart of Liverpool One in a beautifully converted 18th Century warehouse is the unique Catalonian restaurant, deli and bar, Lunya. A true family owned, independent restaurant run by local couple Peter and Elaine Kinsella who left successful careers in education and the health service to pursue their dream.

Lunya opened in 2010 after Peter made a business trip to Barcelona in 1999 and fell in love with the city and its food and atmosphere. After many more visits, Peter and Elaine finally realised their ambition of opening a Catalan deli and restaurant.

As the UK's first Catalonian deli and restaurant, Lunya prides itself on sourcing the finest artisan Catalan and Spanish ingredients, as well as the freshest and highest quality local ingredients, to produce the most authentic deli around. The menu provides a wide range of tapas, paella and roast suckling pig - specialising in blending recipes, ideas and ingredients from Spain and the UK together. The award-winning chefs believe in making absolutely everything themselves from superb quality ingredients. Quite simply, the dishes are 'passion on a plate'.

The restaurant has a relaxed and atmospheric ambience that easily transcends the busy breakfast period through to the evening.

The deli is crammed with Spanish goodies and is a tourist destination in its own right. Wherever you are in the country, you can order any of their products online, with Lunya being the largest online Spanish food website in the country. Lunya is a real foodie's dream.

Relish Restaurant Rewards
See page 003 for details.

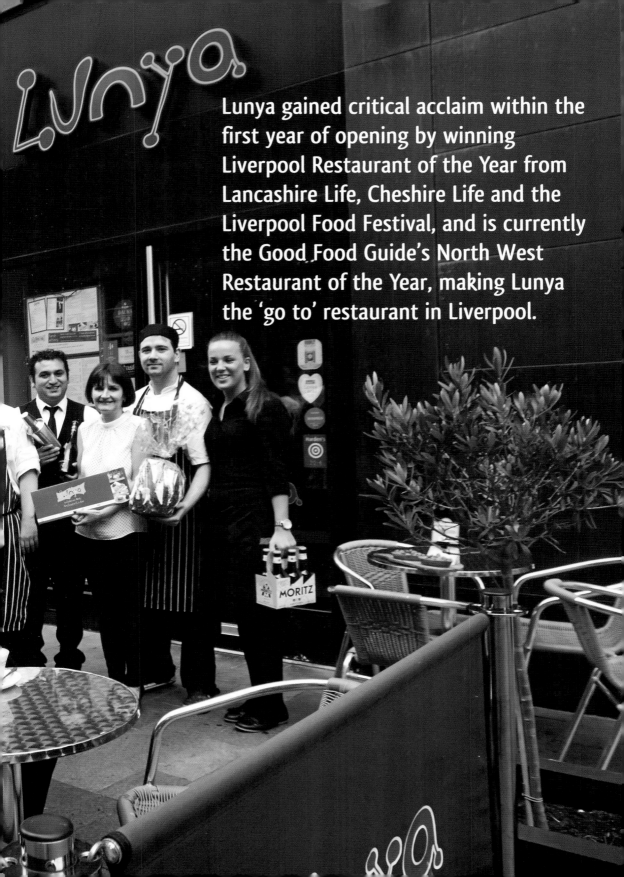

Lunya gained critical acclaim within the first year of opening by winning Liverpool Restaurant of the Year from Lancashire Life, Cheshire Life and the Liverpool Food Festival, and is currently the Good Food Guide's North West Restaurant of the Year, making Lunya the 'go to' restaurant in Liverpool.

CATALAN SCOUSE

SERVES 4

🍷 *Vallemayor Tinto Joven, DOC Rioja*
(Spain)

Ingredients

150g minced beef
20ml olive oil
2 pieces cooking chorizo (picante, sliced into
1cm discs)
2 pieces morcilla (Spanish black pudding, sliced
into 1cm discs)
½ medium sized onion (chopped)
1 clove garlic (chopped)
2 carrots (coarsely chopped)
1kg potatoes (peeled, cut into good sized chunks)
1 sprig thyme
1 bay leaf
400ml vegetable or meat stock
½ tsp pimentón dulce
red wine (splash of)
salt and pepper (to taste)

To Serve

chorizo (halved lengthways and griddled)
parsley (optional)

Method

Fry the mince in a dash of olive oil until just cooked. Add the chorizo, morcilla, onion, garlic and carrots and cook for a further 5 minutes to release all the oils.

Stir in the potatoes, ensuring they get covered with the meat juices. Add the rest of the ingredients, apart from the wine. Stir and leave to gently simmer for at least half an hour. Add the splash of wine. Stir occasionally to break up some of the potato pieces.

It is ready when most of the water has been absorbed, the potatoes are soft and some have started to go mushy. Taste and season with salt and pepper.

Chef's Tip

If you make this dish the day before it will allow time for it to thicken and for the flavours to intensify. Reheat in the microwave until piping hot.

PLUMA IBÉRICA WITH RED ONION CHUTNEY, SHALLOT & BEER PUREE

SERVES 4

Formiga, DO Priorat (Spain)
Full bodied Catalan red.

Ingredients

4 x 200g pieces pluma Ibérica
salt and pepper

Red Onion Chutney

1kg red onions (sliced)
½ red chilli (finely sliced into rings,
including seeds)
40ml vegetable oil
400g sugar
black pepper (pinch of)
1 tsp salt
100ml sherry vinegar
200ml red wine
1 bay leaf

Shallot Purée

2 tbsp olive oil
25g salted butter
400g shallots (peeled, thinly sliced)
100ml Estrella Damm (or similar beer)
4 tbsp double cream
salt and freshly ground black pepper

Method

For The Red Onion Chutney (Prepare ahead)

In a saucepan stock pot, sweat the onions and chilli in the oil, constantly turning to avoid burning and until they start to become translucent (about 30 minutes). Add the sugar, salt and pepper, then mix thoroughly, stirring for about 15 minutes until a syrup forms. Add the bay leaf, vinegar and red wine. Simmer on a high heat for about an hour until it starts to thicken. Remove from heat and allow to cool.

For The Shallot Purée

Add the olive oil and butter to a frying pan on a medium heat. When melted, add the shallots and fry for at least 20 minutes until it's translucent and starts to break down. Add the beer and cook for about another 10 minutes until it reduces to a thick syrup. Stir in the cream, then cook for a further 5 minutes. Taste for seasoning. Blitz in a food processor until completely smooth.

To Serve

Oil and season the pieces of pluma. Fry in a hot pan for approximately 3 minutes per side until the meat is medium rare (pluma is always eaten this way). Allow to rest for 2 minutes. Place a small mound of warmed red onion chutney on a plate and a swirl of shallot purée. Slice the pluma diagonally into 6 and arrange over the purée and chutney.

> **Chef's Tip**
>
> Pluma Ibérica is a cut of fresh shoulder meat taken from the acorn fed Ibérico pigs, in Spain. Deep red and marbled with fat, it is like a rib-eye steak. It is available from Lunya, in store or online.

LECHE FRITA

SERVES 4

 Pirineus Gwertztraminer, DO Somontano (Spain)

Ingredients

Leche Frita
500ml full-fat milk
150g sugar
½ lemon (zest of)
4 egg yolks
100g cornflour

To Finish
cornflour (to dust)
egg wash (beaten egg with a splash of milk)
cinnamon
sugar

To Serve
fruit compôte
ice cream
biscuits (crumbed, optional)

10x15cm rectangular dish (lined with greaseproof paper)

Method

For The Leche Frita (Prepare ahead)

Mix the cornflour with 50ml of the milk to form a smooth paste. Set aside. Add all of the other ingredients into a saucepan, then heat gently. When the mixture is warm, add the cornflour paste and keep stirring whilst you bring it to a near boil. Do not allow it to boil. Reduce the heat so that it simmers gently for 10 minutes, stirring all the time so as to ensure it's completely smooth. Remove the lemon zest and pour the mixture into your prepared dish. Refrigerate for at least 6 hours until completely cold and fully set.

To Finish

Cut the set leche frita into triangles, about 5cm each side. Dust in cornflour and then dip into the egg wash. Deep fry at 170°C for approximately 1 minute, until golden on the outside. Dust with cinnamon and sugar.

This dessert should be served hot on the outside and cool on the inside.

To Serve

Serve with a fruit compôte and ice cream.

> **Chef's Tip**
>
> At Christmas, cut the leche frita into Christmas shapes with cookie cutters and serve with warm mincemeat.

176
MARITIME
DINING ROOM

Merseyside Maritime Museum, Albert Dock, Liverpool Waterfront, L3 4AQ

0151 478 4056
www.liverpoolmuseums.org.uk/mdr Twitter: @MerseyMaritime
Facebook: merseysidemaritimemuseum

The Maritime Dining Room is located on the top floor of the Grade I listed Merseyside Maritime Museum, whose collections reflect the vitality and importance of the port of Liverpool and its role in world history. The restaurant's dual aspect views are breathtaking, capturing the city's history, renaissance and regeneration. On the south side, diners look out over the busy Albert Dock with its Grade I listed buildings, ships and boats, while the north side of the restaurant overlooks the UNESCO World Heritage Site and the Museum of Liverpool.

The design of the dining room reflects the Art Deco inspired elegant travel liners that have passed through Liverpool.

The menu, created by head chef Ben Sheeran, celebrates both British and local produce, combining classic flavours with a modern and cultural twist.

The dishes change regularly to reflect the best seasonal flavours, with a wide choice of dishes from light lunches and pâtisserie through to British and local classics. Their delicious and tempting afternoon tea includes modern savouries served alongside delicate pâtisserie and freshly baked fruit scones with homemade conserve and fresh cream.

The restaurant's team are passionate about providing excellent service to diners and delivering great tasting food with skill and flair. Our dedicated team can help you organise your special celebrations which can be hosted in this unique setting.

Relish Restaurant Rewards
See page 003 for details.

Enjoy delicious food, with unrivalled views at the Maritime Dining Room.

BLACK PUDDING, CARAMELISED APPLE, SHEERAN'S BROWN SAUCE

SERVES 12

 Scousers breakfast loose leaf tea

Ingredients

Black Pudding

700g pork belly (diced)
1 litre chicken or pork stock
1 onion, 1 carrot (for stock)
500g blood (dried)
115g oats
100g pearl barley
2½ green apples (skin on, diced)
375g onion (finely diced)
10g mint
12½g parsley
15g spice mix (equal amounts ground pepper, ground coriander, ground cloves)

To Coat The Black Pudding

30g plain flour
1 egg (beaten)
100ml milk
100g Panko breadcrumbs

Sheeran's Brown Sauce

450g green apples (skin on, quartered)
110g prunes (stoned)
120g onion (diced)
450ml malt vinegar
225g brown sugar
3g ground ginger
2g ground nutmeg
2g cayenne pepper

Caramelised Apples

2 green apples (skin on, cored, cut into 12 wedges)
caster sugar (to sprinkle)

Garnish

micro cress

Method

For The Black Pudding

Cook the pork belly in a pressure cooker if you have one. Alternatively, place it in a pan with the onion and carrot, cover with water and boil for around 1-1½ hours. Remove the pork belly and retain 1 litre of the stock (top up with chicken stock to make 1 litre if required). Leave to cool, then dice into ½cm cubes. While the pork is cooking, cover the pearl barley with water and cook until tender, around 20 minutes. Once the stock, barley and pork belly are cool, combine them with the remaining ingredients in a bowl and mix all the elements together. Place in a heatproof mould and boil in a *bain marie* for 25 minutes. The black pudding should reach a temperature of over 80°C, when probed with a thermometer, to ensure it is cooked through. Leave to cool.

To Coat The Black Pudding

Cut the pudding into 36 even portions (3 per serving).

Dust the cubes of pudding in flour, dip them in the egg, followed by the milk and finally roll them in the breadcrumbs. Once the black pudding is coated in breadcrumbs it can be kept for 3 days in the fridge, or frozen until required. It will keep for 5 days in the fridge without the coating.

For The Sheeran's Brown Sauce

Place the apples, onions and prunes into a large pan and cover with water. Cook until tender, then purée. In a separate pan, add the spices, vinegar and sugar, bring to the boil, then reduce by a third. Add the apple and prune mix and cook out until it thickens. Store in sterilised jars.

For The Caramelised Apples

Sprinkle the apple wedges with caster sugar and fry in a hot pan, turning once as they start to caramelise.

To Serve

Pan fry the pieces of black pudding in hot oil until heated through. Swipe the brown sauce on the plate and arrange 3 pieces of black pudding as pictured. Decorate with the caramelised apple and micro cress.

> **Chef's Tip**
> Any leftover black pudding or trimmings can be used to thicken a stew to give it a richness and body.

MONKFISH WITH SESAME, SAFFRON POTATOES, SUMMER VEGETABLES

SERVES 4

Bladen Sauvignon Blanc 2012
(New Zealand)

Ingredients

Monkfish
800g monkfish tail
2 slices bread
60g sesame seeds
olive oil (to fry)

Saffron Potatoes
2 large potatoes
saffron (pinch of)
500ml vegetable stock

Vegetables
500g fresh broad beans
4 spears asparagus
1 shallot (finely diced)
1 clove garlic (thinly sliced)
extra virgin olive oil
1 tbsp soy sauce
2 plum tomatoes

Garnish
2 radishes (finely sliced)

Method

For The Monkfish
Remove the crusts from the sliced bread and blend in a food processor to a fine breadcrumb. Add the breadcrumbs to the sesame seeds in a shallow container. Slice the monkfish into 4 equal portions, then press into the sesame and breadcrumb mix.

For The Vegetables
Pod the broad beans and *blanch* in boiling, seasoned water for 30 seconds. Refresh in iced water to keep the vibrant green colour. Set to one side.

Warm a drizzle of olive oil in a pan and add the garlic and shallot, allowing them to infuse and soften. Set aside to cool.

Remove the broad beans from their skins and stir into the infused oil, then add the soy sauce.

Blanch the whole plum tomatoes in boiling water for 20 seconds then plunge into iced water. Peel off the skin, cut into quarters and remove the seeds. Cut the flesh into large cubes and add to the broad bean and oil mix.

Slice the asparagus and *blanch* in salted water.

For The Saffron Potatoes
Add the saffron to the vegetable stock, bring to the boil, then simmer for 5 minutes. Using an apple corer, cut 8 tubes of potato and cook until just tender in the saffron infused vegetable stock.

To Serve
Warm a small amount of oil in a frying pan and pan fry the monkfish, turning frequently until golden brown.

Reheat the saffron potatoes in the frying pan that the fish was cooked in. Serve with the summer vegetables and garnish with the sliced radish.

> **Chef's Tip**
> This is a really fresh, light main course with an oriental influence. I use broad beans picked from my dad's garden.

ROAST FLAT PEACHES WITH MARZIPAN & CASSIS

SERVES 4

 Vintage Taylors Port 2007

Ingredients

Peaches

6 flat peaches
sugar (to sprinkle)
butter (small knob of)
100g marzipan

Sorbet

6 peaches (chopped)
150g caster sugar
100ml water

Cassis

100ml apple juice
200g blackcurrants
30ml cassis

Photograph © Tomas Adam

Method

For The Sorbet (Prepare the day before)

In a pan, dissolve the sugar and water, then add the chopped peaches. Simmer for 10 minutes until tender. Remove from the heat and blend to a smooth purée. Pour into a freezer proof container and leave to cool. Place in the freezer, stirring every 30 minutes until just frozen.

For The Cassis

Place the apple juice in a pan with all the blackcurrants (reserving 8 for decoration), then cook out for 20 minutes before blending to a smooth consistency. Stir in the cassis and chill until required.

For The Peaches

Cut the peaches in half and remove the stone. Place them in an ovenproof dish, sprinkle with the sugar and dot with the butter. Grill them for 10 minutes, depending on their ripeness, until they start to colour.

To Serve

Cut the marzipan into cubes and grill until golden. Assemble as pictured, or be creative!

Chef's Tip

Be creative with your food and take influence from all your experiences. For me, it's about childhood memories and recreating wonderful tasting dishes that my mum makes.

186 MEREWOOD COUNTRY HOUSE HOTEL

Windermere, Cumbria, LA23 1LH

01539 446 484
www.merewoodhotel.co.uk Twitter: @LDCHotels

After just one meal at the Merewood Country House Hotel, we are sure that you will see why we were awarded the title 'Lakeland Hotel of the Year' in the Lancashire, Cheshire and Lake District Food and Drink Awards 2013.

At Merewood, you can enjoy a real taste of the Lake District. Head chef Leon Whitehead and his team design inspirational menus using only the very best seasonal and locally sourced ingredients. We take this commitment very seriously, and in addition to using seasonal herbs, fruits and vegetables grown in our gardens or foraged from our grounds, we also rear our own sheep and Highland cattle in the hotel estate to provide the freshest and highest quality meat for our menus. For Leon Whitehead, attention to detail is key. Everything is freshly prepared in our kitchen, from fresh bread to handmade after dinner chocolates.

Whether you choose to enjoy a short break, celebrate a special occasion or merely dine with us at the Merewood, you will benefit from our location set in a secluded estate overlooking Lake Windermere and the local fells. As soon as you step through the front door of our beautiful country house, you'll discover an oasis of comfort, style and relaxation. It's our job to make you feel at home, and our informal and friendly service is so good you'll hardly notice it.

Relish Restaurant Rewards
See page 003 for details.

Under the guidance of head chef Leon Whitehead, Merewood was awarded the prestigious title of 'Lakeland Hotel of the Year' at the Lancashire, Cheshire and Lake District Life Food and Drink Awards 2013.

CITRUS CURED SALMON, SWEET PICKLED FENNEL, DILL MAYONNAISE, CUCUMBER & LIME JELLY

SERVES 4

🍷 *Gewürztraminer, Hugel et Fils, Alsace (France)*

Ingredients

Cured Salmon
500g salmon (skin on)
250g course sea salt
250g caster sugar
10g white peppercorns (crushed)
25g coriander seeds (crushed)
1 lemon (zest and juice of)
1 orange (zest and juice of)
1 lime (zest and juice of)
1 bunch dill

Sweet Pickled Fennel
2 bulbs fennel (sliced as thinly as possible)
200g sugar
50ml white wine vinegar
1 lemon (zest and juice of)
200ml water

Dill Mayonnaise
3 egg yolks
20g English mustard
20ml white wine vinegar
600ml rapeseed oil
lemon juice (to taste)
salt and pepper (to taste)
20g parsley (chopped)
50g dill (chopped)

Cucumber And Lime Jelly
500ml cucumber juice
2 limes (zest and juice of)
5 leaves gelatine (soaked in cold water)

Garnish
leaves
black caviar, salmon Keta caviar

shallow tray (lined with cling film)
large ring mould

Method

For The Cured Salmon (Prepare 24 hours in advance)
Mix together all the cure ingredients, excluding the dill. Score the skin of the salmon and lay onto a large double sheet of cling film on a tray. Cover the salmon with the salt mix, wrap in the cling film and chill in the fridge for 24 hours, turning after 12 hours. Rinse away the salt cure and pat dry. Cover the flesh side with the dill.

> **Chef's Tip**
> Only use the freshest fish, the taste will be much better.

For The Sweet Pickled Fennel (Make 12 hours in advance)
Bring all the ingredients to the boil, add the fennel and remove from the heat. Refrigerate for 12 hours before using.

For The Dill Mayonnaise
Place the egg yolks, mustard and vinegar into a blender. Turn on and add the oil in a slow trickle. When the mayonnaise is ready, add the chopped herbs, lemon juice and salt and pepper to taste.

For The Cucumber And Lime Jelly
Heat the lime juice, add the gelatine then stir into the cucumber juice. Pour into a shallow tray lined with cling film and refrigerate until set - about 2 hours. Cut into cubes.

To Serve
Remove the skin from the salmon and slice thinly. Using a large ring on a plate, fill with sliced salmon, slightly overlapping. Garnish with all the other elements, some fresh leaves and the fish eggs.

BALLOTINE OF SMOKED 'LORDS LOT' PHEASANT, TOASTED PEARL BARLEY, ARTICHOKE & BLACKBERRY GASTRIQUE

SERVES 6

*Vat 10 Pinot Noir, Deen De Bortoli
(Australia)*

Ingredients

Pheasant Ballotine

3 whole cold smoked pheasants
15 rashers thinly sliced streaky bacon
75g chicken breasts
75ml double cream, 25g butter
2 long shallots (finely diced, cooked)
100g mixed wild mushrooms (finely diced, cooked)
50g golden raisins (chopped)
50g cooked chestnuts (finely chopped)
50g pistachios (toasted, chopped)
50g dried cranberries
10g each parsley, chervil, thyme (chopped)
salt and pepper

Sauce

bones from pheasants
20ml sherry vinegar
100ml Madeira
500ml brown chicken stock
sprig thyme, salt and pepper

Blackberry Gastrique

125g granulated sugar
15ml water
65ml cider vinegar
250ml red wine (reduced by half)
250g blackberries

Toasted Pearl Barley

200g pearl barley
600ml chicken stock
thyme, salt and pepper

Artichoke Purée

300g Jerusalem artichokes (peeled, sliced)
500ml chicken stock
50ml double cream, 50g butter

Method

For The Pheasant Ballotine

Blend the chicken and pass through a tamis, fold in the cream, then place in the fridge to chill. Remove the breasts and legs from the pheasants. Dice the thigh meat. Combine all the ingredients, except the breasts and bacon, with the chicken, mix and season. Place 5 pieces of streaky bacon on a double layer of cling film. Place a pheasant breast on top and add a layer of the stuffing, followed by another pheasant breast. Roll up the pheasant in the bacon and cling film as tightly as possible. Tie both ends and repeat 2 more times. Poach in a pan of simmering water for 20 minutes. Remove from the cling film and brown in butter in a hot pan. Allow to rest for 10 minutes.

> **Chef's Tip**
> Use hen pheasants as the meat is more tender.

For The Sauce

Brown the bones in a large saucepan. *Deglaze* with the vinegar, then add the Madeira and thyme. Reduce by half, add the stock and simmer. Skim, check seasoning and pass through a fine sieve.

For The Blackberry Gastrique

Caramelise the sugar with the water and add the vinegar. Add the reduced red wine and boil for 2 minutes. Add the blackberries and remove from heat.

For The Toasted Pearl Barley

Toast the barley in a non-stick pan over a medium heat for about 4-6 minutes. Combine all the ingredients and simmer for 30-35 minutes until the barley is soft.

Artichoke Purée

Place the artichokes in boiling stock and simmer until very soft. Drain, then blend with the butter and cream. Season and pass through a fine sieve.

To Serve

Slice each ballotine into 2. Warm all the elements and plate how you wish.

ENGLISH STRAWBERRIES & CREAM

SERVES 8

🍷 *Prosecco, Frassinelli, Valdobbiadene*
(Italy)

Ingredients

Clotted Cream Parfait

5 egg yolks
85g granulated sugar
85ml water
125g white chocolate (melted)
420g clotted cream

Strawberry Sorbet

500g strawberries
1 lime (zest and juice of)
200g caster sugar

Strawberry Infusion

500g strawberries (diced)
50g sugar

Strawberry Jelly

3 leaves gelatine (softened in cold water)
250ml strawberry infusion
lime (squeeze of)
1 vanilla pod (scraped)

To Serve

500g strawberries (diced)

20x30cm tray

Method

For The Clotted Cream Parfait (Prepare ahead)

Boil the sugar and water until 117°C. Whisk the egg yolks on full speed, pour the boiled sugar onto the egg yolks, whisking until the mix is cool. Fold in the melted chocolate and then fold in the cream.

Pipe the parfait with a 20mm nozzle along a sheet of cling film leaving a gap at each end. Roll the cling film around the mix and roll into a tight cylinder. Tie the ends and place in the freezer.

To Make The Strawberry Sorbet (Prepare ahead)

Blend all the ingredients and pass through a fine sieve. Churn in an ice cream machine and place in the freezer.

For The Strawberry Infusion

Place the ingredients in a vac pac bag and poach at 80°C for 1 hour. Strain the liquid and reserve. Alternatively, place the strawberries and sugar in a bowl, cover with cling film and place over simmering water.

For The Strawberry Jelly

Line your tray with acetate and spray with non-stick spray.

Combine the vanilla, lime and strawberry infusion and heat in a pan until warm. Add the softened gelatine, then allow to cool. Pour on the tray and refrigerate for 1 hour to set.

> **Chef's Tip**
>
> Use 3g of agar agar instead of gelatine to make the dish vegetarian.

To Serve

Remove the parfait from the cling film. Cut the jelly the same width and roll around the parfait. Place on top of the diced fresh strawberries, along with the sorbet.

196

MICHAEL CAINES RESTAURANT AT ABODE CHESTER

Grosvenor Road, Chester, CH1 2DJ

01244 347 000
www.abodechester.co.uk Twitter: @ABodechester

With wonderful views of the surrounding countryside, this is a special place to come to enjoy Michael Caines' cuisine of the highest order. The atmospheric dining room can accommodate 76 diners comfortably indoors, while the outside terrace provides the best open-air dining option in the city, directly overlooking Chester's famous racecourse. Service is friendly and efficient without being overly formal. A glass-fronted, temperature controlled wine room is a feature for more than 150 wines on the ABode Chester list.

Formerly of The Bath Priory, Gidleigh Park and Rick Stein's Seafood Restaurant, Thomas Hine took on the role of executive chef at ABode Chester in 2012.

Tom has worked diligently, rising through the ranks at a number of highly acclaimed restaurants. The Bath Priory as sous chef was his first introduction to Michael Caines' cuisine and his teachings.

An opportunity then arose to learn directly from Michael at Gidleigh Park, a privilege only awarded to chefs with exciting potential. Here Tom learnt the importance of using fresh, locally sourced ingredients and he acquired skills which allowed him to hit the ground running in his own spectacular and reputable kitchen at the Michael Caines Restaurant at ABode Chester.

 Relish Restaurant Rewards
See page 003 for details.

Located on the fifth floor, the Michael Caines Restaurant is the spectacular centrepiece of the ABode Chester, offering a fine dining experience.

PAN FRIED RED MULLET, PROVENCAL VEGETABLES, BASIL OIL, TOMATO VINAIGRETTE

SERVES 4

 Corbières Rosé 2012, Château Ollieux Romanis, Languedoc (France)

Ingredients

Fish
4 red mullet fillets (skin on, pin boned)
oil (for frying)
lemon juice (spritz of)

Tomato Vinaigrette
100ml tomato sauce (make using fresh tomatoes, garlic, thyme, bay leaf)
50ml olive oil
10ml sherry vinegar
5g tomato concentrate

Basil Oil
10g basil
100ml olive oil

Provençal Vegetables
4 cherry tomatoes
4 baby bell peppers
4 violet artichokes
200ml olive oil (to *confit*)

Garnish
basil shoots

Method

For The Tomato Vinaigrette
Place all ingredients into a food processor and blend until *emulsified*.

For The Basil Oil (Prepare ahead)
Add basil into the oil and warm to approximately 80°C. Blitz in a food processor then pass through a fine sieve and chill.

For The Provençal Vegetables
Preheat the oven to 140°C.

Roast the peppers for 30 minutes until the skins blister, then peel.

Blanch, refresh and peel the tomatoes.

Peel and *confit* the violet artichokes - immerse them in the oil, cover with a lid and place in the oven for 1 hour at 120°C.

To Cook The Fish
Trim the fish so it looks neat and tidy, then double check there are no pin bones left in the fish. Season the flesh.

Fry the fish, skin-side down, until crisp and golden brown and then, when you are confident it's about a minute away from being ready, flip the fish over to finish the cooking process. Add a little lemon to finish.

To Serve
Arrange on the plate as shown in the photograph. Dress with basil shoots.

> **Chef's Tip**
> If you don't have a non-stick pan, you can lightly flour the skin to stop it sticking to the pan.

ROAST FILLET OF LANCASHIRE BEEF, SMOKED BACON LARDONS, WILD MUSHROOMS, SHALLOT CONFIT, MADEIRA JUS

SERVES 4

Fairview Pinotage 2011, Paarl
(South Africa)

Ingredients

Fillet Of Beef

600g piece of beef (seasoned on both sides)
10g butter
5 sprigs thyme
4 cloves garlic (crushed)

Madeira Jus

500g beef trimmings
20ml unscented oil
10g butter (unsalted)
50g shallots (sliced)
50g button mushrooms (sliced)
20ml sherry vinegar
truffle marinade (optional)
300ml Madeira
20ml cream
500ml dark chicken stock
5 sprigs thyme
2g white peppercorns
1 bay leaf
2 cloves garlic (crushed)

Shallot Confit

200g shallots (chopped)
100g butter
1 sprig thyme
10g wholegrain mustard
5g garlic purée
5g tarragon (chopped)
salt and pepper (to season)
20ml cream

Garnish

100g wild mushrooms (*sautéed*)
200g spinach (wilted)
8 button shallots (peeled, roasted)
100g cured pancetta (cubed, fried until crispy)
parsley sprigs (deep fried until crisp)

Method

For The Madeira Jus

In a large roasting tray, heat the oil on the hob. Add the beef trimmings, seal well, then add the butter and caramelise until lightly brown. Add the shallots and sweat without colouring, then add the sliced mushrooms and sweat until slippery in look. *Deglaze* with the sherry vinegar and reduce to nothing. Pour in the Madeira and truffle marinade (if using). Reduce by half then add the remaining ingredients. Bring to the boil, transfer to a saucepan, bring back to the boil, skim and simmer for 45 minutes to 1 hour. Pass through a colander and then a *chinois*.

For The Shallot Confit

Melt the butter in a saucepan and add the chopped shallots and thyme. *Confit* slowly, without colouring, for 30 minutes stirring from time to time, adding a drop of water when needed. Strain off the excess butter and finish with the rest of ingredients.

To Cook The Beef

Preheat the oven to 180°C.

Tie the beef to keep its shape. Fry the steak on both sides in an ovenproof pan until golden brown. Add a little butter, thyme and garlic to give a bit more flavour. Place the beef in the oven for 3 minutes, then turn it over and give it another 3 minutes. Take it out the oven and leave to rest for at least 5 minutes.

> **Chef's Tip**
> Take the meat out of the fridge 30 minutes before cooking to let the meat come up to room temperature.

To Assemble The Dish

Carve the beef into 2 pieces per person, then build all the other components around it to make it look pretty. Finish with the Madeira *jus* and parsley crisps.

CHOCOLATE & CONFIT ORANGE MOUSSE, CONFIT ORANGE SORBET

SERVES 4

🍷 Recioto della Valpolicella 2010, Torre del Falasco,
Veneto (Italy)

Ingredients

Confit Orange

4 oranges (lightly scored, being careful not to
penetrate flesh)
4 litres stock syrup

Sorbet

200g confit orange
400ml orange juice
150ml orange stock syrup (from confit)
1 lemon (juice of)

Mousse

120g egg yolks (approximately 6 egg yolks)
50ml stock syrup
100ml stock syrup (heated to 120ºC)
320g dark chocolate (melted)
600ml whipping cream (semi whipped)

Candied Zest

2 oranges (peeled, chiffonade)
200ml stock syrup
icing sugar (to coat)

4 x dessert ring moulds

Method

To Confit The Oranges (Prepare ahead)

Blanch from cold water to the boil and repeat 10 times.
Simmer, in the stock syrup, for 12 hours on a very low heat,
or in the oven at 110ºC.

For The Sorbet (Prepare the day before)

Place the orange, orange juice and orange stock syrup in
a blender.

Blend to a fine coulis and adjust the texture and taste with
the lemon juice. Pass through a chinois. Churn in an ice cream
machine and set in the freezer.

For The Mousse

Place the egg yolks into a bowl with the 50ml of stock syrup
and, using a balloon whisk, cook to a sabayon over a
bain marie, whisking constantly. Once cooked, place into the
bowl of a mixer and whisk in the 100ml of heated stock syrup.
Continue to whisk until cold. Stop the mixer, add the melted
chocolate and about one third of the cream, whisk in until
smooth and then fold in the rest of the cream. Pour into the
dessert ring moulds and set aside in the fridge until needed.

For The Candied Zest (Prepare the day before)

Blanch and refresh the orange peel in hot water 10 times. Cook
in the stock syrup until nice and soft, approximately 30 minutes.

Drain the zest, coat in icing sugar and put in a warm place until
it has dried out, ideally leaving it overnight. Store in an airtight
container until required.

To Serve

Arrange as pictured and enjoy.

> **Chef's Tip**
>
> The method used here is about getting volume from the
> sabayon to give you a velvety texture in the mousse.

206
MICHAEL CAINES RESTAURANT AT ABODE MANCHESTER

107 Piccadilly, Manchester M1 2DB

0161 247 7744
www.abodemanchester.co.uk Twitter: @ABodemanchester

The Michael Caines Restaurant, situated next to the Champagne Bar at ABode Manchester, located in an atmospheric lower level dining room within the former cotton mill building, serves exciting and innovative European cuisine utilising the best local and regional produce and ingredients from Manchester, Lancashire, Cheshire and surrounds. Just descending the stairs makes it feel exclusive and the atmosphere is laid back and relaxed. The Michael Caines Restaurant is one of Manchester's best, loved by locals and buzzing every night of the week.

The wine list has been carefully chosen to complement the cuisine, with a selection of excellent and amazing-value wines from both classic European vineyards as well as New World estates.

Robert Cox became ABode Manchester's new executive chef in 2012 having earned an excellent reputation at ABode Exeter.

Robert has flourished at the Michael Caines Restaurant at ABode Manchester which is well known as the longest standing and consistently successful fine dining restaurant in Manchester.

Originally studying Hospitality Management at Manchester Metropolitan University where he earned a BA, Robert realised he wanted to become a top chef after eating in several renowned Michelin starred restaurants.

Robert established a solid foundation to his career having come from Michael Caines' stable of chefs and he continues to build on this by creating food at ABode Manchester that never fails to reach new, outstanding levels.

Relish Restaurant Rewards
See page 003 for details.

Fine dining, created by Michael Caines MBE, is at the heart. and soul of every ABode. Creating stunning Michelin-star cuisine of the highest order; producing modern, accessible foods at all levels that are simply delicious.

RISOTTO WITH FROGS' LEGS, CRAYFISH, SNAIL, NETTLES & WILD GARLIC

SERVES 4

🍷 *Sancerre 2011, Henri Bourgeois, Loire Valley (France)*

Ingredients

Crayfish And Frogs' Legs
12 crayfish tails (*blanched* for 15 seconds, then plunged in iced water and peeled)
olive oil (to fry), 10g tarragon (chopped)
salt and pepper (to season)
4 breaded frogs' legs (frozen)

Nettle And Wild Garlic Purée
4 small shallots (sliced)
30g butter, 300g spinach (raw)
75g wild garlic (cooked, refreshed)
150ml cream, 30g nettles (picked), 16g garlic purée

Risotto
200g risotto rice, 40g mushrooms (diced)
60g snails (diced)
200ml 50/50 chicken stock and water
60g *confit* onion
20ml snail cooking bouillon, 25g grated Parmesan
120g nettle and garlic purée
20ml extra virgin olive oil

Wild Mushrooms
8 each of Shimeji, Pied Blue, Girolle, Morels and St George mushrooms
butter (knob of), lemon juice (spritz of)

Crayfish Bisque
2kg crayfish carcasses (crushed, chopped small)
1 litre olive oil, 30ml cognac
100g each carrots, onions, fennel (chopped small)
5g whole white peppercorns
½ bulb garlic (cut in half)
250g tomatoes (chopped), 75g tomato paste
400ml water, 1 bay leaf, 5 sprigs thyme
butter (knob of), lemon juice (to taste)

To Garnish
tarragon oil, watercress shoots
groundnut vinaigrette (1 part white wine vinegar to 3 parts groundnut oil, salt and pepper)
tarragon (deep fried), parsley (deep fried)
snail shell, mushroom powder

Method

For The Nettle And Wild Garlic Purée
In a steel pan, sweat the shallots in the butter without colouring. Add the spinach and nettles and continue to sweat until the spinach is cooked. Place into a blender with the *blanched* wild garlic and garlic purée. Bring the cream to the boil and add to the blender. Blend until smooth, season to taste. Cool over ice.

For The Risotto
Put the rice in a pan and cook for 3-4 minutes on a high heat with the mushrooms, snails, bouillon, *confit* onion, 50/50 stock and half the purée. Cook until *al dente*, then finish the risotto with the remaining purée, Parmesan and olive oil.

For The Wild Mushrooms
Cook the wild mushrooms in foaming butter until they begin to colour, then add a few drops of lemon juice.

For The Bisque
Preheat the oven to 200ºC.

Pour 800ml olive oil into a roasting tray and heat. Add the carcasses, roast for 30 minutes. Remove from the oven and *deglaze* with cognac.

Meanwhile, slowly sweat the carrots, onions, fennel and garlic in the remaining 200ml oil in a saucepan, without colouring, for 10 minutes. Add the herbs and sweat for 5 minutes. Add the water, tomatoes and paste. Bring to the boil, cook for 10 minutes.

In a large saucepan, add firstly the carcasses with the oil, then the compôte of vegetables. Add water to just below the level of the carcasses and bring to the boil, reduce to a simmer and cook for 20 minutes. Pass through a colander, then a *chinois*. Reduce quickly to taste. *Monté* with butter and lemon juice to taste.

For The Frogs' Legs And The Crayfish
Deep fry the frogs' legs in a deep fat fryer (160ºC) for 5 minutes. Season lightly. Pan fry the crayfish for 20-30 seconds in a hot pan with olive oil, a pinch of tarragon, salt and pepper.

To Serve
Dress the watercress shoots in groundnut vinaigrette. Place a flat layer of risotto on your plate, top with the frogs' leg, crayfish and mushrooms. Finish with the watercress, tarragon oil, snail shell, the deep fried herbs and finally complement with the bisque and a dusting of mushroom powder.

> **Chef's Tip**
> Make sure you have all your preparation done before you go to finish the dish. It is quite complex and you could get caught out.

LAKE DISTRICT HERDWICK LAMB, BOULANGERE POTATO, CONFIT SHOULDER, FENNEL PUREE & TAPENADE JUS

SERVES 4

🍷 *Chateauneuf-du-pape 2010, Clos St Michel, Rhone Valley (France)*

Ingredients

4 x 100g lamb loin
butter and chicken fat (for frying)

Provençal Crumb
250g breadcrumbs, 125g parsley (picked)
12g garlic, salt, pepper (mixed together)
Bind the above with 50ml olive oil

Lamb Tapenade Sauce
2½kg lamb carcasses (chopped small, roasted at 180°C until golden)
100ml olive oil, 200g onions, 200g leeks
200g carrots (chopped small)
1 bulb garlic (cut in half)
10g fresh thyme, 1g cumin seeds
cinnamon (pinch of), 10g fresh rosemary
500g plum tomatoes (ripe), 100g tomato purée
1½ litres chicken stock, 500ml veal glace

Tapenade Purée (Blitz ingredients)
1 clove garlic, 2 anchovy fillets
150ml olive oil, 100g black olives

Confit Shoulder
500g lamb shoulder (braised), 250g butter
1kg onions (finely chopped), 10g thyme

Boulangère
1 large Desirée potato (sliced into 3mm lengths)
olive oil (for frying), 1 sprig rosemary

Fennel Purée
600g fennel (chopped small)
200ml chicken stock, 200ml water, 5g salt
money bag of muslin: 5g cardamom seeds
5g white peppercorns, 4g fennel seeds
4g cumin seeds

Dijon Pesto (Blend all ingredients together)
18g basil leaves, 4g thyme (picked)
30ml olive oil, 30g Dijon mustard

Fricassée
3 small Girolles, 4 pieces fennel (diced)
30g broad beans, 30g peas
5g mint (chopped), 30ml mint oil

Method

To Make The Lamb Tapenade Sauce
Sauté the onions, leeks, garlic and carrots in the olive oil. Add the thyme, cumin seeds, cinnamon and rosemary. Sweat for a further 5 minutes. Add the tomatoes and tomato purée and cook out for 10 minutes.

Place the bones into a saucepan, add the vegetables, 300ml of water, veal glace and chicken stock. Bring to the boil, reduce to a simmer and cook out for 30 minutes. Pass through a colander and then a *chinois* and reduce to a sauce consistency. Pass through muslin.

For The Confit Shoulder
Sweat the onions in butter until very soft, then add the thyme and cook for 2 minutes, combine with the lamb shoulder meat and mix well. Roll between sheets of greaseproof paper to 2mm thickness and chill. When cool, cut into rectangles, approximately 6x4cm.

For The Potato Boulangère
Overlap 4 slices of potato per person, pan fry in oil until crisp and golden. Cool. Place a rectangle of *confit* shoulder between the potato layers, trim the edges. Cook in the lamb sauce with rosemary for 20 minutes. Reheat in oven (180°C) when ready to serve.

To Make The Fennel Purée
Put all the ingredients in a pan and bring to the boil. Cook for 30 minutes until very soft, remove the money bag, then blend until smooth. Serve hot.

For The Fricassée
In a small pan, heat a knob of butter until it foams and cook the Girolles with a splash of lemon juice, season. Add the beans, peas, fennel, mint and a good splash of mint oil.

To Finish The Dish
Bring the lamb sauce to the boil. Whisk in some tapenade purée to taste. Leave to stand then strain before serving. Season the lamb. Roast on top of the stove with butter and chicken fat. Seal all around and cook to medium rare. Brush lightly on one side with the Dijon pesto and Provençal crumb. Grill to cook the crumb without colouring. Serve as pictured with *blanched* baby fennel, fennel shoots and balsamic reduction.

> **Chef's Tip**
> Turn the lamb in the pan every 20 seconds. Rest it for the same amount of time you cooked it. This will result in juicy, evenly coloured meat.

DUO OF CHOCOLATE, HAZELNUT & MILK CHOCOLATE PARFAIT, WHITE CHOCOLATE ICE CREAM

SERVES 8

Rutherglen Muscat NV, Stanton and Killeen, Victoria (Australia)

Ingredients

Milk Chocolate And Hazelnut Parfait

Pâté à Bombe
12 egg yolks
150g caster sugar
60ml water

Italian Meringue
300g egg whites (approximately 10)
150g glucose, 150g sugar, 60ml water

Parfait
400g hazelnut praline milk chocolate
(melted over a *bain marie*)
300ml whipped cream
50ml Frangelico
200g milk chocolate pistols (chopped)
250g hazelnut nougatine (chopped)

Dark Chocolate Mousse
275g dark chocolate (melted)
750ml double cream
150g sugar
3 whole eggs

White Chocolate Ice Cream
1 litre full-fat milk
100g sugar
10 egg yolks
400g white chocolate (melted over a *bain marie*)
50g milk powder
200ml whipping cream

Garnish
8 tempered chocolate teardrops (made from
200g dark chocolate)
8 dipped hazelnuts (50g sugar)
100 candied hazelnuts (200ml stock syrup)

acetate (8 strips 5 x 20cm)
8 stainless steel mousse rings

Method

Tempered Chocolate Teardrop (Prepare ahead)
Melt half the chocolate by giving it a 20 second burst in the microwave until it gets to 48ºC. Add the other half and allow to reduce to 28ºC, stirring extremely gently. Return to the microwave for 5 second bursts to bring it up to 31ºC. The chocolate will now be tempered. Spread the chocolate onto the acetate strips, bring the 2 ends together to create a teardrop shape. Place in a round mousse ring to set the shape. Freeze.

Dipped Hazelnuts
Bring the sugar to a caramel (155ºC). Using cocktail sticks, dip the peeled hazelnuts into the warm caramel. Allow the caramel to drip in a long shard until it sets. Reserve.

Candied Hazelnuts
Place the hazelnuts into the stock syrup and bring the temperature up to 110ºC. Drain and deep fry at 180ºC until golden brown.

Milk Chocolate And Hazelnut Parfait (Prepare ahead)
Make the *pâté à bombe* first. Mix together the sugar and water and bring to the boil. Cook until 120ºC. Pour into the whipped egg yolks and continue whisking until cool. Remove from the bowl and place into a large mixing bowl.

Now make the Italian meringue by cooking the sugar, glucose and water together until 120ºC. Meanwhile, whip the egg whites to stiff peaks, then, still whipping, carefully pour the heated sugar mix onto the egg whites. Whip until cool.

Add the melted hazelnut chocolate to the *pâté à bombe* mix, with the Frangelico. Fold in the whipped cream and then the Italian meringue. Sprinkle in the chopped milk chocolate and the hazelnut nougatine, then fold in. Place into a piping bag and fill the chocolate teardrops with the mixture. Freeze. Remove acetate prior to serving and top with as many hazelnuts as you can fit on.

For The Dark Chocolate Mousse
Bring the cream to the boil, then pour it over the eggs and sugar. Pour this over the chocolate and whisk to combine. Decant into small bowls and set in the fridge for 1 hour.

White Chocolate Ice Cream
Cream together the egg yolks and the sugar until white and stiff. In a saucepan, combine the milk, milk powder and cream and bring to the boil. Pour some of the milk onto the creamed eggs and sugar, whisking continuously. Return the mixture to the saucepan and, over a medium heat, cook out to 85ºC. Strain through a *chinois*, then pour in the melted white chocolate. Churn in an ice cream machine.

To Finish
Paint a stripe of melted chocolate onto the plate and serve as pictured.

216
MILLER HOWE

Rayrigg Road, Windermere, LA23 1EY

01539 442 536
www.millerhowe.com

Built as a private residence in 1916, Miller Howe is idyllically situated overlooking Lake Windermere with panoramic views of the Langdale Pikes beyond.

The hotel was taken over by the Ainscough family in 2006. Over the last few years the hotel has been sympathetically renovated and refurbished. A lovely new bar area has been added, and the kitchens extended and remodelled. The result enhances this lovely Arts and Crafts building, with William Morris print wallpapers, quirky period furniture, interesting fabrics and an eclectic, ever expanding art collection. In essence we are all about comfortable stylish interiors, attentive friendly service, indulgent food and of course, unforgettable views.

Miller Howe has always been a food destination with John Tovey setting the standards in the seventies. Recently appointed Matt Horsfall now runs the kitchens. The emphasis is on using locally sourced seasonal produce. The style is modern English with a bit of a twist. We also boast an ever changing, diverse wine list to complement Matt's dishes. Miller Howe is open daily for breakfast, lunch, terrace snacks, afternoon tea and dinner.

Relish Restaurant Rewards
See page 003 for details.

Miller Howe is set in five and a half acres of beautiful grounds with gardens stretching towards to the shores of Lake Windermere.

RED PRAWN, MANDARIN PUREE, ALMOND CRUMB

SERVES 4

 The Rude Mechanicals Ephemera, Keith Tulloch 2012 (Australia)
A blend of Pinot Gris and Viognier, a real pot pourri of tropical magic.

Ingredients

Almond Crumb

200g whole almonds (*blanched*)
1 tsp coriander seeds

Mandarin Purée

500ml mandarin purée
5g agar agar
¼ tsp xanthan gum

Boudin Noir

2 boudin noir sticks (or 250g black pudding)
crépinette (to wrap)

Prawn Sauce

8 large red prawns (in shells)
1 tsp tomato purée
20ml brandy
1 litre chicken stock
10ml milk
10ml cream
½ tsp lecithin
½ lemon (juice of)

Garnish

12 mandarin segments (peeled)
12 sprigs baby coriander

Method

For The Almond Crumb

Preheat the oven to 180°C (fan).

Spread the almonds on a baking tray, roast for 10 minutes and leave to cool. On another baking tray, toast the seeds under the grill until golden. Combine in a food processor and blitz a few times until coarsely chopped.

For The Mandarin Purée

Place the mandarin purée and the agar agar in a heavy bottomed pan. Bring to a simmer, whisking continuously until the powder has dissolved. Transfer into a flat container and leave to set in the fridge for about an hour. Once set, transfer to a blender and purée until smooth with the xanthan gum.

For The Boudin Noir

Peel the sticks of boudin noir. Place them in a mixing machine with a paddle and beat until smooth. Transfer onto cling film and roll into a long thin sausage. Place in the freezer for one hour, then portion into 4. Remove the cling film and wrap in crépinette. Seal the ends quickly in a hot pan. Place onto a baking tray ready for heating. When ready to serve, preheat the oven to 180°C and cook the boudin noir for 3 minutes.

For The Prawns And Prawn Sauce

Remove the heads and outer shell of the prawns, then remove and discard the waste pipes from the prawns. Place the heads and shells into a hot pan, crushing down with the back of a spoon. Once brown, add the tomato purée and cook for a further few minutes. Add the brandy and cook until reduced, then add the chicken stock. Reduce by half, crushing the shells until fully broken. Pass through a muslin cloth and reduce by half again. Once reduced, add the milk, cream, lecithin and lemon juice. Use a blow torch to cook the prawns.

To Serve

Serve as pictured.

Chef's Tip

Scorching the prawns with a blow torch adds extra flavour.

CHICKEN WITH BROAD BEAN PUREE

SERVES 4

 Adobe Organic Merlot 2012, Rapel Valley
(Chile)

Ingredients

Chicken Breasts

4 chicken breasts (reserve the skin)
bunch thyme (picked)
30g butter
salt (to season)

Chicken Balls

1 chicken breast (reserve the skin)
2 chicken legs (*confit* - cover the legs with oil,
add salt, garlic and thyme. Cook in the oven at
130°C for 3½ hours)
10ml cream
20g flour
30ml egg and milk mix
20g breadcrumbs

Broad Bean Purée

400g broad beans (peeled)
20ml cream

Madeira Cappuccino

100ml Madeira
100ml chicken stock
10ml cream
¼ tsp lecithin

Girolles

100g girolles
100ml chicken *jus*

Crispy Chicken Skin

reserved skin from chicken breasts
5ml truffle oil
fresh truffle (sliced, to garnish)

Vegetables

100g broad beans (peeled, *blanched*)
100g fresh peas (*blanched*)
4 spears asparagus (chargrilled)
4 spring onions (chargrilled)
½ lemon (spritzed over vegetables)

Method

For The Chicken

Lay each breast on a separate piece of cling film. In the centre,
add a small knob of butter, a pinch of salt, and a sprinkling of
thyme. Roll it up and tie at both ends. Place in a water bath at
58°C for 35 minutes, then roast in a hot pan. Alternatively, seal
the breasts in a hot pan and cook at 180°C for about 15 minutes.

Chicken Balls

Thinly slice the breast then purée in a blender until smooth.
Add the cream and a pinch of salt and blend again until it comes
together to form a mousse. Thoroughly fold in the chopped
confit chicken legs. Divide the mousse into 4 balls. Place each ball
onto a square of cling film and wrap well. Add the wrapped balls
into a pan of boiling water, remove from the heat and leave to
cool in the water. Remove the cling film, then roll the balls in
flour, followed by the egg mix and finally the breadcrumbs. Finish
in a deep fat fryer at 180°C for 1½ minutes. Season.

For The Broad Bean Purée

Cook the broad beans for 1 minute in salted, boiling water.
Drain well then transfer them to a blender with the cream.
Blitz until smooth, season.

For The Madeira Cappuccino

Add Madeira to a hot pan and reduce to a syrup. Once reduced,
add the chicken stock, followed by the cream and lecithin,
then blitz.

For The Girolles

Trim the bottom few millimetres from the girolles. With the
back side of a knife, scrape the outer layer off the stalk.
Bring the chicken *jus* up to the boil, then add the girolles.
Cover with cling film and leave to cool. Reheat when serving.

For The Crispy Chicken Skin

Preheat the oven to 180°C (fan).

Lay the chicken skins flat on a tray with baking parchment.
Brush with the truffle oil, season, then add a few thin slices of
fresh truffle. Cover with another layer of parchment and a
heavy tray. Bake for 20 minutes until golden and crispy.

To Serve

Serve as pictured.

> **Chef's Tip**
> Chargrill the spring onions and asparagus for extra flavour.

CHEESECAKE, BLACK OLIVE PUREE

SERVES 8-10

🍷 *La Cuna de la Poesia Rosada Rioja 2013 (Spain)*
Summer in a glass! Refreshing big strawberry
flavours mingle with vanilla with a smooth
long finish.

Ingredients

Base

250g digestive biscuits (crushed)
300g Hob Nob biscuits (crushed)
250g unsalted butter (browned)

Filling

10 egg yolks
160g sugar
580g cream cheese
130g mascarpone

Jelly Topping

400g strawberries
200ml apple juice
10g vegetarian gel

Black Olive Purée

100g black olives
100g sugar
100ml water
¼ tsp xanthan gum

Strawberry Purée

500g strawberry purée
5g agar agar
¼ tsp xanthan gum

To Serve

small tub vanilla ice cream
1 punnet basil cress
100g strawberries

20cm tart case

Method

For The Base

Gently melt the butter in a pan, warming it slowly. Remove from the heat when it turns golden brown. Add the Hob Nobs and digestive biscuits and bind together. Press into the bottom of a tart case.

For The Filling

Preheat the oven to 110°C.

Whisk the egg yolks and sugar to *sabayon*. Whisk the cream cheese with the mascarpone, then add to the *sabayon*. Pour on top of the pressed biscuit base and bake until firm with a slight wobble for 25–30 minutes. Leave to cool.

For The Jelly Topping

Place the strawberries in a heavy bottomed pan with the apple juice. Bring to the boil then remove from the heat and cool. Bring it back to the boil again, then allow to cool naturally. Once cool, pass through a fine sieve and add the vegetarian gel. Pour the jelly on top of the cooled cheesecake and leave to set for 5 minutes in the fridge or until ready to portion.

For The Black Olive Purée

Add the black olives, water and sugar to a pan. Bring to the boil and reduce the liquor by half. Transfer to a blender, then add the xanthan gum and purée until smooth.

For The Strawberry Purée

Add the strawberry purée and agar agar into a pan and bring to the boil. Simmer for about 2-3 minutes until the powder has dissolved. Transfer to a plastic container and set in the fridge for about 1 hour. Once set, add to a blender with the xanthan gum and purée until smooth.

To Serve

Arrange as pictured and enjoy!

> **Chef's Tip**
>
> Any leftover biscuit base can be used as a bed for the ice cream. To help release the cheesecake from the tart case, gently warm the case with a blow torch.

226
NUTTERS
RESTAURANT

Edenfield Road, Norden, Rochdale, OL12 7TT

01706 650 167
www.nuttersrestaurant.co.uk Twitter: @nuttersofficial

Nutters Restaurant is housed in the lavish grounds of an 18th Century manor house; six and a half acres of groomed parkland with spectacular views across Ashworth Moors, Greater Manchester and beyond. It is the perfect setting for the extravagance and elegance of Andrew Nutter's cuisine. His cooking is unique; an indulgent explosion of the senses that is based on the very best of local and regional produce which is exemplified by Andrew's stunning, award-winning dishes.

Despite the wider success of Andrew's cooking, Nutters Restaurant has remained very much a family affair. Jean Nutter, Andrew's mum, does the accounts and administration whilst his dad, Rodney Nutter, looks after both the management of the business and the restaurant's wines and spirits operation.

The main restaurant seats 150 diners with additional dining in the private rooms accommodating up to 120 guests, providing the perfect venue for Civil Wedding Ceremonies, cocktail parties and lavish receptions.

Whether it's a light lunch, romantic dinner or sumptuous afternoon tea, a Nutters meal is always an experience of interesting flavours and unusual combinations, but above all it's a meal to be enjoyed in beautiful surroundings, safe in the confidence of the quality of the ingredients and the attentiveness of the staff.

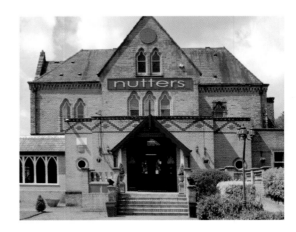

Relish Restaurant Rewards
See page 003 for details.

Great honest food, letting the true flavours of the local produce shine. The Nutters experience - not just a meal but a culinary adventure.

HONEY ROAST DUCK SALAD, CONFIT FRITTER WITH ORANGE & GINGER DRESSING

SERVES 4

Chassagne Montrachet, Domaine Bouchot-Ludot 2011 (France)
Plummy, redcurrant and tobacco hint on the nose with a fullish body and soft, velvety tannins.

Ingredients

1 x 1½kg whole duck (breasts and legs removed)

Duck Confit Fritter

2 duck legs
100ml goose fat
1 tbsp olive oil
½ red chilli (finely chopped)
1 clove garlic (finely chopped)
1 tsp fresh root ginger (chopped)
4 spring onions (finely chopped)
4 spring roll pastry sheets
1 egg (beaten)
vegetable oil (to deep fry)

Honey Roast Duck Breast

2 duck breasts
2 tbsp runny honey
1 tsp poppy seeds
1 tsp sesame seeds
1 small pineapple (cut into 3cm dice)
25g butter

Orange And Ginger Dressing

2 oranges (peeled, pith removed, cut into segments, juice reserved)
1 tsp fresh root ginger (finely chopped)
2 tsp Dijon mustard
1 tbsp sherry vinegar
3 tbsp extra virgin olive oil

To Finish

baby shoots
duck crackling shards

Method

For The Duck Confit Fritter

Preheat the oven to 120°C.

Place the duck legs in a small deep roasting tray, cover with the goose fat and place in the oven for 3 hours, until the meat is tender and flakes off the bone. Leave to cool.

Heat the olive oil and fry the chilli, garlic, ginger and spring onions for 2 minutes until softened.

Remove the meat from the duck legs (reserve the skin) and combine with the spring onion mix. Season to taste.

Place one quarter of the mixture at the bottom of each sheet of the spring roll pastry. Brush the sides with beaten egg and roll to form a cylinder.

To Make The Duck Crackling

Preheat the oven to 180°C. Place the reserved duck skin on a tray and bake for 8-10 minutes until golden and crispy. Set aside.

For The Honey Roast Duck Breast

Preheat the oven to 180°C.

Place the duck breasts, skin side down, into a dry, hot pan. Cook for about 3 minutes until golden, turn over and cook for a further 2 minutes. Pour off any excess fat and add the honey, poppy and sesame seeds. Baste the duck with the honey until it starts to caramelise. Transfer the duck to an oven tray and roast for 6 minutes. Remove from the oven and leave to rest. Add the pineapple to the duck pan. Heat gently and add the butter, coating the pineapple in any remaining honey and seed mix.

Chef's Tip

Watch how far you caramelise the honey in the pan. Too far and the glaze will go bitter and be unpalatable.

For The Orange And Ginger Dressing

Place the reserved orange juice in a small pan with the ginger. Bring to the boil and reduce until 2 tablespoons remain. Remove from the heat and add the Dijon mustard. Whisk in the vinegar and oil. Season to taste.

When Ready To Serve

Heat the vegetable oil to 180°C. Deep fry the fritters until golden, hot and crispy. Cut each fritter into 3 even slices.

Cut the rested duck breast into 3mm slices. Arrange the pineapple, duck and fritters on 4 plates. Drizzle over the dressing and finally finish with a flourish of baby shoots and duck crackling shards.

PAN SEARED WILD SEA BASS, JERSEY ROYAL GRATIN, ENGLISH ASPARAGUS WITH A CHIVE & LEMON HOLLANDAISE

SERVES 4

Waterkloof Circle of Life, Stellenbosch (South Africa)

Ingredients

Jersey Royal Gratin

500ml whipping cream
1 clove garlic (finely chopped)
1 sprig rosemary (chopped)
500g baking potatoes (peeled)
300g Jersey Royals (washed)
3 carrots (peeled)
50g Gruyère cheese (grated)
50g Kirkham's Lancashire cheese (grated)

Chive And Lemon Hollandaise

3 egg yolks
1 tbsp lemon juice
1 tbsp white wine vinegar
115g butter (bubbling hot)
2 tsp fresh chives (chopped)
salt and ground black pepper

Sea Bass

4 x 115g wild sea bass fillets (skin on, boned)
1 tbsp olive oil
2 cloves garlic (cut into wafer thin slices)
4 cloves fermented black garlic (cut into wafer thin slices)
2 lemons (zest and juice of)
3 tbsp extra virgin olive oil
1 tbsp chives (chopped)

To Finish

2 bunches English asparagus (peeled, *blanched*)
heritage carrot balls (*blanched*)
4 sprigs fresh basil
girolles (*sautéed*)
edible flowers

15 x 25cm deep tray (lined with non-stick paper)

Method

For The Jersey Royal Gratin (Prepare the day before)

Preheat the oven to 130ºC.

Heat the whipping cream in a casserole pan. Add the garlic and rosemary and reduce by half. Season to taste.

Slice the potatoes and carrots into 2mm thick slices. Layer the vegetables into the prepared tray, interlayered with the cream and cheeses.

Cover with foil and bake in the oven for 1½ hours until cooked through. Remove from the oven. Place a tray on top and a weight on top of that. Leave overnight in the fridge.

Slice the gratin into 12x3cm rectangles. Place on a tray ready to be reheated. When you are ready to serve, place the gratin into a preheated oven, 180ºC, for 8 minutes to heat through.

For The Chive And Lemon Hollandaise

Place the egg yolks into a food processor, then add the lemon and vinegar. Pulse a few times, then slowly pour in the hot butter as you mix on a high speed for 30 seconds. Stir in the chives. Season to taste.

For The Sea Bass

Heat the oil in a non-stick pan and seal the sea bass, skin-side down, for 3 minutes until lightly coloured. Turn over and cook for a further 2 minutes.

In a small pan, warm both garlics, lemon, oil and chives. Spoon on top of the fish.

To Serve

Warm through the *blanched* asparagus and lay on the plates, top with the gratin and spoon around the hollandaise. Finally, top with the sea bass, a scattering of the carrot balls, a sprig of fresh basil, the *sautéed* girolles and edible flowers.

Chef's Tip

Any remaining garlic marinade can be kept in the fridge for a good few days and is ideal for pouring over king prawns for a quick marinade that packs a punch.

LEMON MERINGUE & BLACKCURRANT PANNA COTTA

SERVES 4

Moscato Passito, Araldica (Italy)
Unctuous and rich, yet always refreshing. With
cool fruit characters of elderflower, honey, lemon
and chamomile.

Ingredients

Meringue
125ml egg white
225g caster sugar
vanilla extract (splash of)

Panna Cotta
1 litre whipping cream
½ lemon (zest of)
1 vanilla pod (split)
200g caster sugar
3 leaves gelatine (soaked)
50g fresh blackcurrants

Lemon Curd
4 egg yolks
2 whole large eggs
100g caster sugar
120ml lemon juice
85g unsalted butter

To Finish
4 caramel discs
blackcurrant ice cream
lemon sorbet
chocolate decorations
sugar decorations
mint leaves

4 glasses

Method

For The Meringue (Prepare the day before)

Whisk the egg whites in a clean bowl until light and fluffy. Slowly add the caster sugar until it forms stiff peaks. Stir in the vanilla.

Pipe the meringue into droplet peaks on to non-stick paper. Place into a warm cupboard, or in your oven on the lowest setting, overnight to dry.

For The Panna Cotta

Warm the cream, lemon zest and vanilla in a small pan. Add the sugar and gelatine and stir until dissolved.

Remove the vanilla pod, then divide the mixture in half. Blend the blackcurrants into one half and pass both through sieves, keeping them separate.

Pour the plain lemon mixture into the 4 glasses and place in the fridge for 1 hour to set.

Once set, pour the blackcurrant panna cotta on top and return to the fridge for a further hour.

For The Lemon Curd

Combine the egg yolks, whole eggs and sugar.

Melt the butter and lemon juice together in a small pan, then pour in the egg mixture. Stir continuously over a low light until smooth and thickened.

When Ready To Serve

Top the panna cotta with a few teaspoons of lemon curd, or pipe it around the edges of the glass. Add the lemon sorbet and meringue droplets.

Working quickly, top with a caramel disc, and with a blow torch, melt the sides so it completely encases the glass. Top with a scoop of blackcurrant ice cream, a flourish of chocolate and sugar decorations and mint.

> **Chef's Tip**
>
> Half an hour before serving, ball your ice cream and place back into the freezer. It firms up more giving you vital extra minutes when assembling the finished dish.

236
PLANET PAVILION CAFE

Jodrell Bank Discovery Centre, University of Manchester, Macclesfield, SK11 9DW

0161 306 9591
www.themoderncaterer.co.uk www.jodrellbank.net

Jodrell Bank hosts the latest venue from The Modern Caterer which was originally established in 2005 by award-winning chef Peter Booth. Peter has been cooking his simple, fresh, seasonal food for Mancunians and the international community alike for over 10 years now. Born in Liverpool, Booth travelled from an early age to London, Europe, the Americas and Middle East, exploring local foods and cultures along the way. His experiences are reflected in the tantalising range of innovative, flavoursome dishes. 'Good food speaks for itself', says Booth, 'simplicity and flavour are key'.

In 2010 Booth opened the doors at Jodrell Bank, home to the world famous Lovell Telescope, set in the heart of rural Cheshire. Since then, the team has built up a firm and loyal following at the Planet Pavilion Café, with a reputation for providing excellent service, backed up by expertly sourced local and regional produce.

The recipes that follow are inspired by The Modern Caterer's event business and developed by head chef Paul Partridge. They are centred round the ever popular monthly Lovell lecture series. Paul is instrumental in providing high quality and creative catering for all kinds of corporate and private events.

Relish Restaurant Rewards
See page 003 for details.

Committed to delivering delicious food and great service, The Modern Caterer recognises its responsibility to the environment, and is devoted to the ethical sourcing of local and sustainable, seasonal produce. They want to share their passion with you!

ARTICHOKE & WHITE TEA SOUP, CRISPY EGG YOLK & BORAGE

SERVES 4

 Nook's Yard Cheshire Perry

Ingredients

Artichoke Soup
700g Jerusalem artichokes (peeled in lemon water, thinly sliced)
1 leek (white of, diced)
2 sticks celery (diced)
2 cloves garlic (crushed)
2 tbsp olive oil
50ml dry white wine
1 tbsp sherry vinegar
1 tbsp sugar
1 sprig thyme (picked)
1 lemon (zest and squeeze of)
1 star anise
600ml vegetable stock
3 white tea teabags
4 tbsp double cream

Crispy Egg Yolk
4 eggs
100g Panko breadcrumbs
plain flour
salt and pepper

Garnish
borage flowers

Method

To Make The Artichoke Soup

Sweat off the whites of the leek with the celery and garlic in the olive oil without colouring. When softened, add the white wine, vinegar, sugar, thyme, along with the zest of the lemon and star anise and reduce by half. Add the artichokes, stock and teabags. Simmer until the artichokes are soft, about 10 minutes. Cook for as short a time as possible to get the best flavour from them. Remove the teabags. Stir in the cream, season, then blend until smooth and pass through a sieve. Add a squeeze of lemon juice.

For The Crispy Egg Yolk

Separate the eggs and freeze the yolks on a plate covered with cling film.

Once frozen, season the flour and coat the egg yolks in flour. Dip the yolks into the beaten egg white, followed by the breadcrumbs.

Deep fry at 180°C for 1 minute until golden. You still want the yolk to be runny.

To Serve

Garnish with the borage flowers and serve as pictured.

Chef's Tip

The egg yolks, once they are coated in Panko (Japanese breadcrumbs), can be left to defrost in the fridge before cooking.

PAN ROAST BRILL, PICKLED VEGETABLES, PEA MOUSSE, GARDEN PEA SALAD, ANISE SAUCE

SERVES 4

 Chenin Blanc, Grand Cape
(South Africa)

Ingredients

Brill
4 x 170g brill portions (skin on)
butter (knob of)
lemon juice (spritz of)
salt and pepper

Pea Salad
50g *blanched* fresh peas (chilled and
lightly crushed)
50g sugar snap peas (cut lengthways)
40g pea shoots
lemon juice (spritz of)
olive oil (drizzle), salt and pepper

Pickled Vegetables
200g mixed vegetables (baby fennel, baby
turnips, carrots)
100g caster sugar
100ml white wine vinegar, 100ml water
1 large red chilli (deseeded and *julienned*)
1 star anise
1 clove garlic (lightly crushed)
1 tbsp fresh ginger (grated), 1 stick cinnamon
1 tsp fennel seeds, ½ tsp cumin seeds
salt and freshly cracked black pepper

Pea Mousse
300g fresh peas
1 leaf gelatine (soaked)
sugar (pinch of), salt and pepper
100ml double cream (half whipped)

Anise Sauce
50ml white wine vinegar
2 tbsp soy sauce, 2 tbsp honey
50ml olive oil, 25ml rapeseed oil
1 tbsp lemon juice, 2 star anise (ground)

4 lined ramekins or container

Method

For The Pea Salad
Combine the fresh peas, sugar snaps and pea shoots in a bowl. Drizzle over a little olive oil, a spritz of lemon juice and seasoning to taste.

For The Pickled Vegetables
Slice the vegetables, leaving some carrot tops whole, season with salt, then leave to stand for about 1 hour. Wash the salt off the vegetables and drain well.

Place all the other ingredients in a pan and simmer for 10 minutes. Pour the pickling liquor over the vegetables and allow to cool.

For The Pea Mousse
Cook the peas in boiling, salted and sugared water for 4 minutes. Drain, reserving the cooking water, then refresh in iced water.

Using a hand blender, or in a liquidiser, blend the peas with the gelatine and 75ml of the cooking water until smooth. Pass through a fine sieve.

Semi set the pea mixture in the fridge so that it is still soft but firm enough to hold the cream. This will depend on the temperature of your fridge so check the mixture regularly. Fold in the cream, then spoon the mixture into lined ramekins or container, then return to the fridge to set fully, about 1 hour.

Chef's Tip
Cut the pea mousse with a hot knife.

For The Anise Sauce
Simply whisk all the ingredients together.

To Cook The Brill
Pan fry the brill, skin-side down, in a hot pan. When the skin is crispy, after 1 or 2 minutes, turn over the brill, add the butter, a little seasoning and a squeeze of lemon juice.

To Serve
Serve as pictured.

CARAMEL & HAZELNUT CUSTARD, BURNT HONEY SPONGE, BEES POLLEN & MANGO

SERVES 4

🍷 *A single espresso from our single origin organic coffee beans!*

Ingredients

Caramel Custard
160ml double cream
50ml full-fat milk
30g hazelnut paste
62g egg yolk
70g caster sugar
80g caramel chocolate (broken into pieces)

Hazelnut And Honey Sponge
40g honey
75g ground hazelnuts
75g self-raising flour
75g soft light brown sugar
90g caramel chocolate (broken into chunks)
75ml milk
75ml vegetable oil
1 medium egg

Mango Sauce
1 ripe mango (peeled, stoned)
1 vanilla pod (seeds of)
½ lemon (juice of)
caster sugar

Hazelnut Tuiles
100g fondant icing
50g honey
50g isomalt
50g hazelnut paste

Mango Foam
½ of the mango sauce (see above)
1 tbsp caster sugar
1 tsp egg white powder
½ tsp xanthan gum

Garnish
bees pollen
mango (cubed, caramelised)
edible flowers

450g loaf tin (lined or greased)

Method

For The Caramel Custard
Boil the cream with the hazelnut paste and milk. Combine the egg yolk and sugar in a bowl. Slowly pour the liquid into the egg mix. Cook in a *bain marie*, stirring constantly, until the temperature reaches 83ºC. Place the chocolate into a bowl, pour the custard over the chocolate and mix together. Cover and bake for 40-45 minutes at 98ºC in a combi or in a water bath. Leave to cool, then freeze for about 4 hours until set.

For The Hazelnut And Honey Sponge
Preheat the oven to 170ºC (fan).

Heat the honey in a pan until it caramelises.

Mix all the dry ingredients together. In a separate large bowl, mix all the wet ingredients together with the caramelised honey. Add the dry ingredients to the wet and mix together until smooth. Bake for 10-15 minutes in the prepared loaf tin.

To Make The Mango Sauce
Blend the mango flesh with vanilla seeds and lemon juice until smooth. Sweeten to taste.

For The Hazelnut Tuiles
Preheat the oven to 160ºC (fan).

Place all the ingredients in a pan and heat gently until it has all dissolved. Allow to cool.

Spread the mixture as thinly as possible onto a non-stick mat and bake for 10-12 minutes until it bubbles. Leave to cool on the tray. Break into shards and keep in an airtight container.

For The Mango Foam
Whisk all the ingredients until it is light and fluffy.

To Serve
Serve as shown, dusted with the bees pollen.

> **Chef's Tip**
> Bees pollen is a superfood readily available from health food shops.

246
THE PUNCH BOWL INN & RESTAURANT

Crosthwaite, Lyth Valley, Cumbria, LA8 8HR

01539 568 237
www.the-punchbowl.co.uk Twitter: @Punchbowlinn

The Punch Bowl Inn & Restaurant, Crosthwaite is situated in the heart of the delightfully unspoilt Lyth Valley countryside next door to the Parish Church of St Mary's. The history as an Inn dates back as far as 1829 when it was also used as a blacksmiths.

Our aim today is to provide you with a traditional English pub feel but, after major renovations in 2005, we can now offer you more luxurious, sumptuous surroundings. The stunning valley views from some of our nine individually designed bedrooms capture the heart of the valley and its abundance of damsons and damson blossom in the springtime.

The outdoor terrace is a perfect place to enjoy lunchtime dining or, if staying with us, your complimentary cream tea. In colder months enjoy dining or relaxing by the log fires. Friendly, attentive staff, fine food, local real ales and an impressive wine list have our guests returning again and again.

Our award-winning 2 AA Rosette menus, created by head chef Scott Fairweather, are served all week in both dining rooms; one a more contemporary style space and the other a cosy low beamed dining area with a traditional pub atmosphere.

Scott is now enjoying his third year with us, having won Young Chef of the Year in his first two consecutive years. He is dedicated, passionate, creates inspiring menus and is keen to showcase the best of the area, always using locally sourced seasonal food. The young kitchen team has been with him for over two years and together they constantly strive to deliver and maintain very high standards; enticing customers back using a combination of classic flavours with a twist on the 'classics' or traditional homemade food using modern techniques but presented in an honest and exciting fashion.

Relish Restaurant Rewards
See page 003 for details.

The Punch Bowl's aim for all our guests is to create a home away from home where they can relax, unwind and be well and truly spoiled.

CRAB MOUSSE, PASSION FRUIT, SAFFRON MAYONNAISE, CRAB RAREBIT

SERVES 4

 Viognier, Casa de Lolol (Chile)

Ingredients

Passion Fruit Jelly

100ml passion fruit purée
40ml water
1 gelatine leaf (soaked in cold water)

Crab Mousse

1 shallot (peeled, finely diced)
1 garlic clove (peeled, sliced)
½ bulb fennel (finely sliced)
1 tbsp vegetable oil
100ml vegetable stock
65ml double cream
150g brown crab meat (passed through a fine sieve)
1 tbsp lemon juice
1 gelatine leaf (soaked in cold water)
15ml natural yoghurt

Saffron Mayonnaise

saffron strands (large pinch of - soaked in 2 tbsp hot water for 10 minutes)
2 egg yolks, 10g Dijon mustard
10ml white wine vinegar, 400ml vegetable oil
salt, lemon juice (to season)

Crab Rarebit (Not pictured)

4 slices granary sourdough bread
25g butter
25g plain flour
100ml Cumbrian ale
150g creamy Lancashire cheese (grated)
1 egg yolk
1 tsp English mustard
4 tsp Worcestershire sauce
1 tbsp crab stock concentrate
cayenne pepper (to season)
freshly ground black pepper (to season)

Garnish

1 passion fruit (seeds scraped out)
12 pea shoots (trimmed)

4 x 70ml *dariole* moulds

Method

For The Passion Fruit Jelly (Allow time for all elements to set)

Bring the passion fruit purée and water to the boil, remove from the heat, whisk in the softened gelatine and pass through a fine sieve. Pour 2 tablespoons into the *dariole* moulds, leave on a flat tray to set in the fridge for 1 hour. Reserve the rest for later use.

For The Crab Mousse

Over a medium heat, sweat the shallot, garlic and fennel in the vegetable oil to soften. Add the vegetable stock and 40ml cream, reduce by a third. Pour into a liquidiser, add the brown crab meat, lemon juice and gelatine. Blend for 3 minutes until smooth, pass through a fine sieve and season to taste. Leave to cool to room temperature, then lightly whip the remaining cream and yoghurt, then fold into the crab. Pour onto the set passion fruit jelly. Leave to set in the fridge for 2 hours.

For The Saffron Mayonnaise

Add the egg yolks, mustard and vinegar into a large, clean bowl with a damp cloth underneath to secure it. Bind together using a balloon whisk, then add a very small amount of the oil until it's well blended. Add a little more oil and continue to whisk thoroughly between each addition until the sauce *emulsifies*. Stop adding the oil when it has reached a very thick consistency. Finish by whisking in the saffron water. This will change the colour, taste and also loosen the mayonnaise.

For The Crab Rarebit (Not pictured)

Melt the butter in a non-stick saucepan and stir in the flour. Cook over a low heat for 30 seconds, stirring constantly. Slowly add the beer, simmer for 2-3 minutes stirring constantly until the sauce is thick and smooth. Add the cheese, egg yolk, mustard, Worcestershire sauce, crab concentrate and cayenne pepper. Cook until the cheese melts, stirring constantly. Season with freshly ground black pepper and set aside to cool. Place the bread on a baking tray lined with aluminium foil and toast on each side until golden brown. Spread the cheese sauce thickly over the bread, making sure the slices are completely covered so the edges don't burn. Return to the grill for 20-30 seconds or until lightly browned and bubbling.

Serve as pictured.

> **Chef's Tip**
>
> This dish is perfect for the summer, a lighter lunch option that also looks and tastes good enough to be fit for a dinner party. It reflects simplicity but also creativity and is a staple menu item at the Punch Bowl.

MAPLE GLAZED DUCK, RED CABBAGE, DAUPHINOISE POTATOES, ORANGE JELLY, GOLDEN RAISIN JUS

SERVES 4

🍷 *Vouvray, Cuvée des Fondraux, Didier Champalou (France)*

Ingredients

Duck
2 x 2kg whole Gressingham ducks (breasts removed, skin scored, seasoned with salt and pepper. Legs can be used for another recipe)
4 sprigs thyme, 40g unsalted butter
4 tbsp maple syrup

Orange Jelly
200ml fresh orange juice, 1 bay leaf, 1 star anise
2 cardamom pods (crushed), 2g gellan gum

Golden Raisin Jus
2 duck carcasses (broken into 2-3cm pieces, roasted at 200°C (fan) for 30 minutes)
1 white onion and 2 carrots (peeled, diced)
1 leek (white part only, washed, finely sliced)
2 sticks celery (washed, sliced)
1 head garlic (sliced in half)
2 tbsp vegetable oil
2 star anise, 1 bay leaf (torn), 2 sprigs thyme
500ml red wine, 2 litres beef or duck stock
30g golden raisins, lemon juice (spritz of)

Dauphinoise Potatoes
400ml double cream, 200ml full-fat milk
1 head garlic, 2 sprigs thyme
3 large Maris Piper potatoes (washed, peeled, finely sliced using a *mandolin*)
100g Parmesan cheese (finely grated)

Red Cabbage
2 small heads red cabbage (finely shredded)
2 red onions (peeled, finely sliced)
2 Bramley apples (peeled, cored, diced)
500ml red wine vinegar, 1 litre red wine
250g dark brown sugar
1 cinnamon stick (broken in half)
1 tsp fennel seeds, 2 star anise, 1 bay leaf (torn)

24cm square baking tray (lined)
4 ramekins

Method

For The Orange Jelly
Bring all the ingredients, except the gum, to the boil. Remove from the heat then cling film the pan. Infuse for 20 minutes, then pass through a fine sieve into a clean pan. Bring to a simmer and whisk in the gellan gum until dissolved. Remove from the heat and pour out onto the tray. As it cools, tilt the tray to create a thin, even layer that reaches into the corners. Cool, then cut into 12cm squares. Store between greaseproof paper.

For The Duck
Lay the breasts fat-side down in a cold frying pan and place over a low heat. Allow the fat to slowly render down and crisp up, about 15 minutes, removing the fat from the pan every 5 minutes. Once golden and crisp, turn the duck breasts over and place in a preheated oven with the thyme sprigs at 180°C (fan) for 6-8 minutes (medium rare). Remove from the oven and allow to rest on a wire rack for 4-6 minutes. In the same pan, add the maple syrup and butter and bring to the boil, then glaze the duck breasts. Carve before serving.

For The Golden Raisin Jus
Preheat the oven to 200°C (fan). *Sauté* the vegetables in the oil with the herbs and spices until lightly brown. Add the duck bones to the pan and *deglaze* with the red wine. Reduce by half, then add the stock. Bring to the boil, simmer, skimming off any fat, until reduced so it coats the back of a spoon. Pass through a fine sieve. Add the raisins and leave to plump up. Season before serving with salt and lemon juice.

For The Dauphinoise Potatoes
Gently infuse the cream, milk, garlic and thyme over a low heat for 30 minutes. Pass through a fine sieve, then cool to room temperature. Place the potatoes into the cream. Arrange 2 layers of potato into each ramekin, add a little Parmesan, then cover with the garlic cream. Repeat until the layers reach three quarters of the way up the ramekins. Finish with cream and Parmesan. Place onto a baking tray, cover with greaseproof paper, followed by tinfoil tightly wrapped around the sides of the tray. Bake in a preheated oven at 180°C (fan) for 60 minutes until tender. Remove from the oven, place the ramekins under a hot grill until golden brown.

For The Braised Red Cabbage
Preheat the oven to 180°C (fan). Place all the ingredients into a large roasting tray and cover with tin foil. Cook for 2½ hours, stirring every 30 minutes. Carefully drain the cabbage, reduce the liquid to a thick syrup, then stir back into the cabbage. Season.

To Serve
Serve as pictured.

VANILLA PANNA COTTA, STRAWBERRIES, ELDERFLOWER, HONEYCOMB

SERVES 6

Sauternes, Chateau Briatte
(France)

Ingredients

Panna Cotta

2 vanilla pods (sliced lengthways, seeds scraped)
660ml double cream
100ml semi-skimmed milk
100g caster sugar
3 leaves gelatine (soaked in cold water)

Strawberries

200g strawberries (hulled, quartered)
2 tbsp balsamic vinegar
2 tbsp icing sugar
4 sprigs tarragon
cracked white pepper (large pinch of)

Jelly

285ml elderflower cordial
2 leaves gelatine (soaked in cold water)

Honeycomb

150ml water
140g caster sugar
50g honey
10g bicarbonate of soda

Garnish

30 sprigs micro lemon balm cress

6 glass bowls
1 litre plastic tub (double lined with cling film)

Method

For The Panna Cotta (Allow up to 4 hours to set)

Place all ingredients, apart from gelatine, in a pan. Bring to a simmer, then whisk for 5 minutes to dissolve the sugar. Remove the pan from the heat, squeeze the excess water from the gelatine, then whisk into the cream. Remove the vanilla pods and place the pan onto a bowl of ice. Whisk regularly until cooled to room temperature. Pass through a fine sieve and divide the mix into 6 glass bowls. Set in the fridge for 2-4 hours.

For The Strawberries

Place all the ingredients into a bowl and gently toss together. Cover with cling film and leave in a slightly warm place for an hour. Stir every 15 minutes. The fruit will start to soften and take on the flavours. Drain on kitchen paper before serving.

For The Elderflower Jelly (Allow up to 4 hours to set)

Bring the elderflower cordial to a simmer over a medium heat. Squeeze the excess water from the gelatine and whisk in well. Pass through a fine sieve and pour into the lined container. Leave to set in the fridge for 2-4 hours. Slice into 30 x 1cm squares using a warm, sharp knife.

For The Honeycomb

Line a large baking tray with a silicone mat or greaseproof paper.

Boil the honey, water and sugar in a large, heavy-bottomed saucepan until it turns into a golden caramel. Remove from the heat and whisk in the bicarbonate of soda as quickly as possible, then pour onto the tray. (Once the bicarbonate of soda is added, the caramel will double in size). Allow to cool to room temperature before breaking up into 30 small pieces. Store in an airtight container.

To Serve

Plate as pictured and enjoy this beautiful dish.

Chef's Tip

This is a recipe for all year round; change the garnishes of the panna cotta depending on the seasonality of ingredients. In the late autumn we use mulled wine with cranberries, and in the spring try blood orange and Yorkshire rhubarb!

256
PUSCHKA

16 Rodney Street, Liverpool, L1 2TE

0151 708 8698
www.puschka.co.uk Twitter: @Puschkapeople

A small but perfectly formed bohemian enclave, Puschka's oak panelled dining rooms nestle right in the heart of Liverpool's lovely old Georgian quarter.

Founded in 2001 by partners Glen and Doug, south-enders who began their careers at downtown Nautical Catering College and uptown art school respectively, this romantic little eatery has been making quite a name for itself amongst its fervently-loyal local and not-so-local followers. Described by the Guardian as "a place you do not want to leave", the simple, honest, locally-sourced and homemade food is prepared daily and served up fresh from their tiny subterranean kitchen.

An ever-changing specials board gives the menu a weekly facelift. Friendly and unpretentious service coupled with dishes like potted Southport shrimps with crab claw and mace butter, or balsamic red onion and rosemary marinated lamb rump, provide diners with a comforting taste of home. Alongside top-secret, pop-up events happening all over the North West, their thriving outside catering business delivers fresh food to the great and the good at music festivals nationwide.

Relish Restaurant Rewards
See page 003 for details.

Glen says: "We love cooking, we love eating and more importantly we love the way that food and wine brings friends and family together."

LIVERPOOL GIN CURED SALMON, CUCUMBER JELLY, GIN & TONIC JELLY

SERVES 4-6 (4 good portions, 6 lighter portions)

Les Granges de Felines - Domaine de Belle Mare - Languedoc Roussillon (France)
Refreshing alternative to your traditional Sauvignon Blanc. Delicate flavours which cut through the sharp oiliness of the gin cured salmon.

Ingredients

Salmon

300g piece fresh salmon (skinned, boned)
3 tbsp Liverpool Gin (or similar premium gin)
50g caster sugar
50g good sea salt
2 unwaxed limes (zest of)
2 tbsp dill (chopped)
2 tbsp fennel fronds (chopped)
2 tbsp dried juniper berries (crushed)

Cucumber Jelly

1 cucumber (deseeded)
1 lime (juice of)
1 leaf gelatine (soaked)

Gin And Tonic Jelly

25ml Liverpool Gin (or similar premium gin)
100ml Fever-Tree tonic
1 leaf gelatine (soaked in 100ml water)

Garnish

micro lemon basil

Method

Curing The Salmon (Prepare 24 hours in advance)

Rinse the salmon and remove any loose scales. Trim it, then pat dry with kitchen roll. Soak the salmon in the gin.

Mix the sugar, salt, lime zest, dill, fennel fronds and crushed juniper in a bowl.

Lay out a piece of cling film and coat with the salt mix. Lay the salmon on the salt cure and wrap tightly.

Place in a tray or container and leave to cure in the fridge for 24 hours.

Remove from the fridge and slice finely, 4 nice slices per person is fine for a starter course.

Making The Cucumber Jelly

Blitz the cucumbers with a hand blender or in a food processor and strain through a fine sieve. Add the lime juice to the cucumber juice and mix together. Heat a little of the mix and add the strained gelatine. Set in small moulds or in a tray lined with cling film to a height of around 1cm. Allow at least 2 hours to set.

For The Gin And Tonic Jelly

Mix the gin with the tonic and heat it a little. Add the soaked gelatine and water then stir until dissolved.

Set in small moulds or in a tray lined with cling film to a height of around 1cm for at least 2 hours, or until firm.

To Serve

A lined tray is our preferred choice for setting the jelly. Simply remove the jelly and cut into equal sized cubes before serving with your gin-cured salmon.

Chef's Tip

There's lots to do in this recipe but well-worth the effort to create one of the most popular, tasty and good-lookin' appetisers at Puschka. We've passed this recipe on to countless customers over the years and the variations we get back have led to this latest version. We love the little twist given to the recipe by the inclusion of gin, tonic and cucumber which all marry together so well. Come on, stretch yourself and impress your guests!

COD, CHORIZO POMMES ANNA, SHERRY

SERVES 4

🍷 The FMC, Chenin blanc - Ken Forrester Wines
(Western Cape, South Africa)
Big, bold flavours to enhance the delicate flavours
of the cod. Buttery notes complement the chorizo
pommes Anna.

Ingredients

Cod
4 fillets cod (skin on)
olive oil (for frying)

Pommes Anna
800g waxy potatoes (peeled, washed))
300g chorizo (thinly sliced)
200g salted butter (melted)
salt and pepper

Sherry Sauce
300ml cream sherry
100g salted butter
chorizo (cubed, optional)
1 sprig fresh thyme

To Serve
spinach or curly kale (wilted)

Method

For The Pommes Anna (Allow 5 hours to make)

Preheat the oven to 180°C (fan).

Thinly slice the potatoes using a *mandolin*.

Smear some of the butter around the inside of an ovenproof frying pan. Layer the potatoes in the pan, buttering and seasoning every layer with salt and pepper and adding sliced chorizo to every third layer.

Cover the pan with foil and cook on the hob on a medium heat for 7 minutes. Transfer to your pre-heated oven for 90 minutes.

Remove from the oven, then pierce with a knife to ensure the potatoes are cooked through. Place another pan, of a similar size, on the foil on top of the potatoes and place weights onto the top pan. We normally use a cookbook and large tin of tomatoes combination! You need to use enough weight to press but not crush the pommes Anna. Press for around 3 hours at room temperature, portion as desired and reheat as required, covered in foil.

Cooking The Cod And The Sherry Sauce

Heat a heavy bottomed non-stick frying pan with a little olive oil until nearly smoking. Place the cod fillets in the pan carefully, skin-side down, and cook for around 5 minutes.

Heat the sherry in a saucepan until boiling. *Flambé* the sherry, then add the butter and turn down the heat to a low simmer. Reduce the liquid for about 5 minutes.

We like to add some cubes of chorizo at this point too. It makes a delicious addition to the sauce. Fling in the leaves from your thyme sprig at this point too!

Now turn the cod onto the flesh side and reduce the heat. Add a little butter and cook for a further 3 minutes. Season to taste.

To Serve

Serve the cod as pictured with wilted greens and the pommes Anna. Finish with the fabulously rich sherry and chorizo sauce.

Chef's Tip

We have served up this dish in various guises over the years. Adapted from a dish we enjoyed at a restaurant in a fishing village outside Jerez in Spain, this is its latest, greatest incarnation. The unctuous pimento colours and flavours of chorizo, combined with the sherry and butter, make a fabulous *jus*, which goes particularly well with cod, hake and monkfish. Give them all a go! Pommes Anna is a favourite too. We've made them with *confit* duck, chorizo (as here) and plain. They're all absolutely delicious so make more than you need to, so you can hit them again for a late night snack!

HONEY & PINE NUT TART, OLIVE OIL & SMOKED SEA SALT ICE CREAM

SERVES 4

Patricius Late Harvest Tokaji (Hungary)
Golden, sweet and peachy. A perfect match for the
honey flavours and to soften the saltiness of the
ice cream.

Ingredients

Ice Cream

200ml full-fat milk
140g sugar
100ml double cream
4 egg yolks
160ml extra virgin olive oil
(buy the best you can afford as this will affect
the flavour of your ice cream)
3 pinches good quality smoked sea salt
(or to taste)

Sweet Pastry

340g plain flour (sieved)
110g icing sugar
225g unsalted butter (softened, cubed)
3 egg yolks

Honey And Pine Nut Filling

240g raisins
3 tbsp dark rum
50g plain flour (plus extra for dusting)
175g unsalted butter (softened)
175g caster sugar
175g ground almonds
5 eggs (beaten)
85g pine nuts
2 tbsp clear honey (plus extra for drizzling)

Garnish

extra ripe purple figs
icing sugar (for dusting)

22cm loose bottomed tart or flan tin

Method

For The Olive Oil And Smoked Sea Salt Ice Cream

Bring the milk, sugar and cream to the boil.
In a separate bowl, whisk the egg yolks to a pale, fluffy texture.
Pour the cream mix over egg yolks while whisking continuously.
Leave until cool.
Add the olive oil and smoked sea salt and mix together. Place
the mixture into an ice cream machine and churn to a thick and
creamy consistency. Portion into tubs and freeze. This is best
served when just frozen.

For The Sweet Pastry

Stir the flour and icing sugar together in a mixing bowl.
Beat the butter and slowly add it to the flour mixture.
Add the egg yolks and combine until the pastry comes together.
Cling film the bowl and chill for 30 minutes.
Preheat the oven to 180°C.
On a floured surface, roll the pastry to around 3-4mm thick to fit
your flan tin. Lay the pastry out carefully in the tin and press firmly
into the edges, trimming off any excess. Pierce the base with a
fork. Using baking beans, blind bake your tart case for 8 minutes.
Remove the baking beans and bake for a further 5 minutes.
Remove from the oven and chill. Do not remove the case from
the tin as you still have to bake the tart with its filling!

For The Honey And Pine Nut Filling

Soak the raisins in the rum for 1 hour.
Beat the butter, sugar, flour, almonds and eggs together, then
stir in the soaked fruit. Pour into the tart case (still in its tin).
Scatter over the pine nuts and press them lightly into the
surface, then drizzle with honey.
Return the tart to the oven at 160°C (fan) and bake for 40-45
minutes until firm to the touch. If the top browns too quickly,
cover it loosely with foil.
Allow the tin to cool before removing the tart and portioning it.

To Serve

Serve just-warm with the olive oil and smoked sea salt ice
cream. Dust with icing sugar. Great with extra-ripe purple figs
on the side too!

Chef's Tip

We've been experimenting with ice cream since we opened
Puschka really but this is our favourite flavour to date.
This little combination may appear startling at first but give
it a go. You will be pleasantly surprised - we promise you!
And those olive-y and salty undertones complement the
nutty-sweet tart so well. If you can't find smoked sea salt,
just use a good quality sea salt like Maldon.

266
QUINCE & MEDLAR RESTAURANT

11-13 Castlegate, Cockermouth, Cumbria, CA13 9EU

01900 823 579
www.quinceandmedlar.co.uk

Often considered the 'Weirdos' of the dining world, vegetarians have sometimes been relegated to lower rank status. It is meat or fish that has been the shining star on the plate. But happily over the past few years, things have changed and meat-free cooking has gained increasing recognition and respect in the restaurant world.

Twenty five years ago when Louisa and Colin Le Voi were considering taking over a restaurant that served only vegetarian meals, friends thought they were taking a huge risk, especially as the restaurant was located on the edge of the Lake District where lamb and beef farming is a major activity.

However, the business has proved to be very successful producing creative botanical dishes about which Colin and Louisa have been most passionate. Their food reflects this passion without being too biased towards the common image of vegetarianism.

The Quince & Medlar dining room has a warm, intimate atmosphere, with paintings which are changed frequently, by local artists.

Both Louisa and Colin were born in Cumbria and whenever possible buy their vegetables, fruit, eggs and dairy produce from local suppliers.

Quince & Medlar attracts many non-vegetarians who enjoy good food offered on the varied and interesting menu, finely cooked and presented.

Relish Restaurant Rewards
See page 003 for details.

Discover creative meat free dishes from veg patch to plate served in the Le Voi's intimate listed Georgian town house next to the castle in the West Cumbrian gem town of Cockermouth.

POTTED CRUSHED CHICKPEA, APRICOT & TAMARI PATE, CHEESE SHORTBREADS, SESAME OAT BISCUITS

SERVES 4

🍷 *Viognier, Dominio De Punctum (Spain)*

Ingredients

The Pâté

200g dried chickpeas
1 bay leaf
5-6 dried apricots (chopped)
1 tsp olive oil
1 large red onion (chopped)
2-3 cloves of garlic (crushed)
1 tsp balsamic vinegar
1 tbsp tomato purée
1 tbsp tamari
½ tsp ground cumin
½ tsp paprika
¼ tsp turmeric
1 tsp lemon juice
½ tsp Demerara sugar
salt (pinch of)
ground black pepper

Cheese Shortbreads

100g unsalted butter
50g Parmesan or cheddar (grated)
100g plain flour
50g ground almonds
cayenne pepper (pinch of)
salt (pinch of)

Sesame Oat Biscuits

100g oats
1 dsp sesame seeds
dried mustard powder (pinch of)
salt (pinch of)
bicarbonate of soda (pinch of)
1 tbsp sunflower oil
10–15ml water

4 ramekin dishes

Method

For The Pâté (Start the day before)

Soak the chickpeas in water overnight.

Drain the chickpeas and place in a pan with fresh water and the bay leaf, then cook for 30 minutes.

Add the apricots to the chickpeas. Continue cooking for a further 15 minutes. Drain after cooking but save the liquid and disregard the bay leaf.

Sauté the onion and garlic in the oil for 3-4 minutes, then add the remaining ingredients. Cook for a further couple of minutes.

Crush the cooked chickpeas and apricots in a food processor, then combine with the onion mixture. Add some of the cooking liquid if the pâté seems too dry.

Check the seasoning. Chill in individual ramekin dishes. Allow to come to room temperature before serving.

For The Cheese Shortbreads (Makes 20 biscuits)

Preheat the oven to 190°C.

Grease a baking tray, or line with baking parchment.

Combine all the ingredients in a food mixer until it forms a dough. Place the dough in the fridge for an hour.

Roll the dough into small balls in the palms of your hands and flatten on the tray with a fork.

Chill again for another 20 minutes.

Bake for 20–25 minutes until golden brown.

To Make The Sesame Oat Biscuits (Makes 12 biscuits)

Preheat the oven to 190°C.

Grease a baking tray, or line with baking parchment.

Mix all the dry ingredients together in a bowl then add the oil and enough water to make a soft dough. Roll out to about 4mm thickness and cut into rounds. Bake in the oven for 30-35 minutes.

To Serve

Serve the pâté with the biscuits as shown.

> **Chef's Tip**
>
> Add a few vegetables to the cooking of the chickpeas, then remove them before crushing. If you can't find tamari, use soy sauce.

BUTTERNUT SQUASH WITH SPICED QUINOA, RED PEPPER SAUCE & HAZELNUTS

SERVES 4

 Nero d'Avola
(Sicily)

Ingredients

Butternut Squash

1 large butternut squash (skinned)
paprika (to dust)
salt and freshly ground black pepper

Spiced Quinoa

150g quinoa
500ml vegetable stock
1 tbsp olive oil
1 large red onion (chopped)
3 large sticks celery (diced)
1 courgette (diced)
6 dried apricots (chopped)
2 garlic cloves (crushed)
100g fresh ginger (peeled, finely chopped)
½ tsp cumin
1½ tsp paprika
good splash white wine
handful roasted hazelnuts (chopped)
salt
freshly ground black pepper

Red Pepper Sauce

2 red peppers (roasted, skinned)
300ml vegetable stock
1 small red onion (chopped)
1 small carrot (chopped)
1 celery stick (chopped)
1 tsp olive oil
1 garlic clove (crushed)
1 tsp paprika
salt and ground black pepper (to season)

Garnish

roasted whole hazelnuts
roasted red peppers
wilted greens

Method

A Few Notes About Quinoa

Quinoa is pronounced keen-wah. Although it is eaten like
a grain it is technically a seed. It contains almost twice as much
fibre as other grains. It is a complete protein, meaning
it contains all of the amino acids necessary for our protein
needs. It is naturally gluten free, high in iron and calcium.

For The Butternut Squash

Preheat oven to 200°C.

Divide the squash into 8 equal discs. Dust with some paprika,
season and bake on a tray for about 12-15 minutes until
just tender.

> **Chef's Tip**
> Go for the pointed end of the squash without the seeds.

For The Quinoa

Cook the quinoa in a pan with the vegetable stock. Bring to the
boil, reduce the heat and simmer (with the lid on) for about 10
minutes until the quinoa has fluffed up and the liquid has been
absorbed. Leave to one side.

Fry the onion and celery in a pan with the oil for 2-3 minutes.
Add the courgette, apricots, garlic, cumin, paprika and fresh
ginger. Cook for a further minute or so. Add the wine and
continue cooking for a further 2-3 minutes. Season, then remove
from the heat. Add the chopped hazelnuts.

Combine the onion mixture with the quinoa.

For The Red Pepper Sauce

Heat all ingredients, except the red peppers and stock, gently in
a pan for 3-4 minutes.

Add the peppers, cook for a further minute and then add the
stock. Simmer for 15-20 minutes.

Liquidise and season to taste.

To Serve

Preheat the oven to 200°C.

Lay 4 of the cooked squash discs on a greased baking tray.
Place a large round pastry cutter over the disc and spoon in the
quinoa and onion mixture. Lay a second disc of butternut squash
on the top, then spoon another layer of the quinoa on top.
Pat down gently. Repeat this to make 4 stacks. Finish with a few
whole hazelnuts on top. Cover lightly with foil and bake for
20-25 minutes, until hot. Serve with the roasted red pepper sauce.

RAW COCONUT & LIME TORTE

SERVES 4

🍷 *Muscat de Rivesaltes, Clos Saint Martin*
(France)

Ingredients

The Base

130g macadamia nuts
6 pitted dates

The Filling

200g cashew nuts (soaked overnight)
50ml maple syrup
50g coconut oil
2 large limes (zest and juice of)
salt (pinch of)

To Garnish

toasted coconut chips
raspberries
redcurrants
lime zest

4 x 7cm baking rings

Method

To Make The Base

Line 4 baking rings with greaseproof paper and sit on a baking tray.

Place the macadamia nuts and dates in a food processor and blend until a wet paste is formed.

Divide the paste between the 4 baking rings and press down to form the bases.

Chill in the fridge, until firm, while you make the filling.

To Make The Filling (Allow 4 hours to set)

Drain the cashews and add them to the cleaned bowl of your food processor along with all the other ingredients. Blend for about 5 minutes until light, creamy in colour and smooth.

Pour the cashew and lime mixture onto the bases and chill until ready to serve - at least 4 hours.

To Serve

Decorate with raspberries and redcurrants and top with toasted coconut chips and a grating of lime zest.

Chef's Tip

This is Louisa's recreation of a dessert she tasted in Australia while visiting her daughter. It is unusual because it is dairy free, gluten free and sugar free but it is surprisingly sweet and utterly moreish.

276
ROSSO
RESTAURANT & BAR

43 Spring Gardens, Manchester, M2 2BG

0161 832 1400
www.rossorestaurants.com Twitter: @RossoRestaurant Facebook: RossoRestaurants

Five years into its much-feted existence, Rosso Restaurant and Bar continues to be at the top of the hill of restaurants in Manchester. Situated at the peak of King Street in an incomparable and breathtaking Grade II listed, 19th Century building, Rosso has set out to provide an experience in contemporary yet traditional luxury unrivalled throughout the city.

Famed not only for its famous clientele and ownership, (in case you didn't already know, Rio Ferdinand is the name behind the restaurant), but also for its fantastic Italian food, fine wines and a luxurious bar unparalleled to most outside of London.

What really lies behind Rosso's success is that its doors are open to all. Beyond the glitz, glamour and fantastic menus is the core belief that we have something special here, to be shared and available to all.

 Relish Restaurant Rewards
See page 003 for details.

For head chef Stephen Hildebrandt and his team, the brief is simple - source seasonal, local, fresh ingredients along with authentic Italian products to produce traditional, as well as new trending dishes, which appeal to a broad customer base. And with customers topping 500 daily, it seems to be working.

ROMBO ARROSTO
ROASTED TURBOT ON POTATO PANCAKE
WITH OLIVES & CHERRY TOMATOES

SERVES 2

 Chardonnay Langhe DOC Marchesi Di Gresy
(Italy)

Ingredients

1 x 650g turbot
salt and pepper (to season)

Potato Pancake

2 waxy potatoes (such as Estima)
olive oil (drizzle of)
salt (pinch of)
pepper (pinch of)
2 sprigs thyme (chopped)

Olives And Cherry Tomatoes

50g unsalted butter
125g pitted black Gaeta olives
200g Piccolo cherry tomatoes
50ml dry white wine
extra virgin olive oil (splash of)
1 lemon (squeeze of)

Garnish

6 baby basil leaves

Method

For The Potato Pancake

Preheat the oven 190°C.

Slice the potatoes as thinly as possible, using a *mandolin* or very sharp knife.

Drizzle 2 ovenproof pans with a little olive oil and layer the potato slices over the bottom of the pans.

Season with a pinch of salt and pepper, then evenly sprinkle the chopped thyme over the potatoes. Drizzle over a little more olive oil.

To Prepare The Fish

Remove the head and the fins from the fish. Using a heavy, sharp knife, cut across the backbone of the fish and cut into 2 even pieces. Season with salt and pepper and place both pieces on top of the potato pancakes.

Place both pans in the oven for 15 minutes until the fish is firm to the touch in the centre and the potatoes are golden brown.

> **Chef's Tip**
> You can use any firm white fish in this recipe, such as cod or halibut.

Assembling The Dish

Lift the fish from the pans with a pallet knife. Remove and discard all the skin and bones, keeping the fillets together.

Invert the pancakes onto 2 plates and place the now filleted fish onto the potato pancakes. Keep warm.

For The Olives And Cherry Tomatoes

Place the 2 pans that the potato and fish were cooked in over a medium flame. Divide the butter, olives, cherry tomatoes, white wine and olive oil between the 2 pans and simmer for 2 minutes until reduced and creamy. Finish with a squeeze of lemon.

To Serve

Arrange a potato pancake on a plate and position the turbot fillet on top. Spoon the olives and tomatoes over the fish and garnish with the baby basil leaves.

FILETTO DI MANZO
PAN SEARED HEREFORD FILLET
OF BEEF, ROCKET PESTO & GIROLLE
MUSHROOM SAUTE

SERVES 4

 Barbaresco Camp Gros Martinenga DOCG 2005
Marchesi Di Gresy (Italy)

Ingredients

2 Hereford centre-cut beef fillets
salt and pepper (to season)

Pesto

70g wild rocket
30g basil
30g flat leaf parsley
30g pine nuts (toasted)
2 cloves garlic
50g Parmesan cheese (grated)
100ml extra virgin olive oil
salt and pepper (to taste)

Mushroom Sauté

250g Girolle mushrooms
50ml dry white wine
25g unsalted butter
25ml double cream

Garnish

1 punnet pea shoots

To Serve

Heirloom tomato salad

Method

For The Pesto

Add all ingredients, except the olive oil, to a food processor and blitz for 20 seconds. Slowly drizzle in the olive oil into the mix and season with a pinch of salt and pepper to taste.

You only need a good tablespoon of the pesto for this dish, so refrigerate the rest and use with your favourite pasta. It will keep for a week.

To Cook The Fillets Of Beef

Season the steaks with salt and black pepper. You are going to cook the steaks medium rare. In a hot, heavy bottomed frying pan, with a touch of oil, sear both steaks for 2 minutes on either side until they are a good brown colour. Remove from the pan and let them rest.

For The Mushroom Sauté

Add the mushrooms, butter and white wine to the hot steak pan and stir with a wooden spoon for 2 minutes.

Add a tablespoon of the pesto to the pan and a splash of double cream to bind the mixture slightly.

To Serve

Place a little of the mushroom *sauté* onto warmed plates and place the rested fillets on top. Add the remaining mushroom *sauté* to the top of the fillets and around the plates.
Garnish with pea shoots and serve. This dish goes great with an Heirloom tomato salad.

> **Chef's Tip**
> Any mixed wild mushrooms work well here and the pesto is fantastic with pasta.

BOMBOLONI
ITALIAN RICOTTA FRITTERS, HOT CHOCOLATE DIP WITH VANILLA FOAM

SERVES 4-6

🍷 *Vino Santo Trentino Arele DOC 1999*
(Italy)

Ingredients

Fritters

400g ricotta cheese
3 medium free-range eggs
120g caster sugar
1 lemon (grated zest of)
bicarbonate of soda (pinch of)
3 tbsp sultanas
200g plain flour
500ml vegetable oil
125g icing sugar
1 tsp cinnamon

Dipping Sauce

150g Valrhona 66% dark chocolate
250ml double cream
50g muscovado sugar
150ml full-fat milk
1 vanilla pod (split)

6 cups or dipping pots

Method

To Make The Fritters

Drain the moisture from the ricotta cheese, then place in a large mixing bowl with the eggs and beat until smooth. Add the caster sugar, lemon zest, bicarbonate of soda, sultanas and flour, then stir well to combine the ingredients. Cover with cling film and place in the fridge for 1 hour.

For The Dipping Sauce

Break the chocolate into a large bowl. Add the double cream and muscovado sugar and melt over a pan of simmering water (*bain marie*). Do not stir. When the chocolate has melted, stir and pour into cups or dipping pots and keep warm.

Take a small saucepan and slowly heat the milk with the split vanilla pod - do not boil. Using a hand blender, froth up the vanilla infused milk to a foam and spoon this froth on top of the cups of chocolate.

Cooking The Fritters

Lay some kitchen paper on a tray or large plate.

In a heavy bottomed saucepan, heat the vegetable oil until it sizzles. Using a tablespoon, drop dollops of the dough mixture into the oil a few at a time. Remove when golden brown and place on the kitchen paper to drain the excess oil.

Combine the icing sugar with the cinnamon, place the fritters onto a serving plate and dust with the cinnamon icing sugar. Serve with the chocolate dipping sauce

Chef's Tip

The fritters will keep well in a sealed container for a day so you can enjoy your leftovers with a coffee.

286
SIX30 BAR & BISTRO

630 Liverpool Road, Ainsdale, Southport, PR8 3BH

01704 576 770
www.six30.co.uk Twitter: @SIX30Ainsdale

Situated in Ainsdale village, a short distance from the classic English resort of Southport, lies Six30 Bar and Bistro. Opened in 2012, the Bistro is now firmly established as one of the top restaurants in the area.

Previously an old Victorian house, the property has been stylishly redeveloped to create a warm, friendly and vibrant bar and restaurant. Family owned Six30 Bar and Bistro offers the highest quality modern British food under the guidance of passionate, young head chef, Matt Ellis.

The 50 cover tastefully decorated restaurant with its high ceilings, impressive chandeliers and unique artwork, oozes quality that matches the food being brought to your table. Excellent customer service is at the forefront of the business, but equally as important, is the emphasis that the owners place on their first class service being both casual and informal.

The restaurant offers top end local produce with seasonally changing à la carte menus and fortnightly changing set menus. The venue boasts a large landscaped garden which provides a beautiful backdrop for the outside terrace dining area.

A spacious bar welcomes you into the premises and its combination of wood and rustic stonework provides a warm and inviting atmosphere for pre-dinner drinks or for those who just wish to linger over a drink or two. The venue is also available for hire for functions and special events.

Relish Restaurant Rewards
See page 003 for details.

Six30 is rapidly becoming a real talking point for its excellent food and friendly service in a relaxed environment, with frequently changing menus and gourmet events. The venue is available for private hire for functions and special events.

CURED SALMON, POTATO MOUSSE, BABY WATERCRESS, PICKLED BEETROOTS

SERVES 4

 Jean- Rémy Haeffelin Pinot Blanc, Alsace (France)

Ingredients

Salmon Cure

400g salmon (skinned, pin boned, trimmed)
100g salt
100g sugar
1 lime, 1 lemon, 1 pink grapefruit, 1 orange
(zest of, reserve the juice for vinaigrette)
5 tbsp sel rose (pink salt)

Potato Mousse

225g Ratte potatoes
75ml cream
50ml milk
125ml crème fraîche
2 leaves gelatine (soaked in cold water)
150ml semi-whipped cream
salt (to season)

Baby Beetroots

3 baby golden beetroots
3 baby candy beetroots
3 baby purple beetroots

Vinaigrette For Beetroots

2 tbsp honey
30g caster sugar
juices of all citrus fruits (from salmon cure)
30ml white wine vinegar
10ml cider vinegar
3 tsp wholegrain mustard
100ml olive oil
10ml groundnut oil

Garnish

baby watercress

Method

For The Salmon (Prepare the day before)

Combine all ingredients and cover the salmon with the mixture. Wrap tightly in cling film and refrigerate for 24 hours. Wash off the cure and pat dry.

Cut into 6 x 2.5cm thick strips making sure no blood line (brown) remains on the salmon. Wrap using cling film and tie at each end keeping a tight barrel shape.

Carefully place in the water bath and poach at 46ºC for 9 minutes, then plunge into iced water to stop the cooking process.

For The Potato Mousse

Peel the Ratte potatoes and boil until soft. Drain, then pass through a drum sieve or potato ricer.

Bring the cream and milk to the boil with the crème fraîche, then add the soaked gelatine.

Blend the potato and milk mixture until smooth. Chill down in a bowl over ice. When cold, fold in the semi whipped cream and season.

For The Vinaigrette Dressing

Mix the honey, sugar, citrus juices, vinegars and mustard together. Slowly stream in the oils or *emulsify* with a stick blender.

For The Beetroots (Prepare ahead)

Boil the beets separately until cooked, then chill. Gently rub the skins to remove them. Dress all the beetroots in the dressing in separate bowls.

To Assemble

Carefully remove the salmon from the cling film and brush with the vinaigrette. With a sharp knife, carefully cut in half.

Using 2 hot spoons, *quenelle* the potato mousse onto the plate. Gently arrange the baby beets and salmon. Dress with baby watercress.

Chef's Tip

A water bath is ideal for this dish as it can maintain a correct temperature but it's not essential. An alternative is to poach the salmon gently in olive oil.

ROAST BREAST OF GRESSINGHAM DUCK, CONFIT LEG CANNELLONI, CELERIAC GRATIN, DUCK CRACKLING, SWEET POTATO PUREE

SERVES 4

Domaine Carneros by Taittinger Avant-Garde Pinot Noir (California, USA)

Ingredients

1 whole duck

Salt For Confit Duck

100g Maldon sea salt
4 star anise
2 cinnamon sticks
2 oranges (zest of)
1kg duck fat

Celeriac Gratin

6 large potatoes (sliced 1mm thin on a *mandolin*)
1 large celeriac (sliced 1mm thin on a *mandolin*)
950ml double cream
4 cloves garlic
2 sprigs rosemary

Sweet Potato Purée

2 sweet potatoes (peeled, diced)
35g butter
50ml olive oil

Pasta Dough For Cannelloni

300g pasta 00 flour
3 free range egg yolks
1 tsp salt
2 tbsp olive oil

Garnish

sweet potato crisps
1 bunch asparagus
1 tbsp apricot marmalade

15x25cm baking tray (greased, lined)
5cm ring cutter

Chef's Tip

Salt the duck legs overnight for added depth of flavour.

Method

Salt Duck Confit (Prepare the day before)

Add all salt and spices to a blender and pulse. Cover the legs and refrigerate for 24 hours, then wash off.

Cover with duck fat and bake at 120°C for 4 hours. Carefully remove and chill slightly. Carefully take the skin off and reserve. Flake the meat into a bowl discarding all bones. Roll the flaked meat tightly in cling film to form a small barrel shape. Chill.

The Sweet Potato Purée

Preheat the oven to 150°C (fan).

Place the potato in a small ovenproof bowl, season, add olive oil and mix well. Cover with foil and bake until soft for about 20-25 minutes. Place in a blender with butter and blend until smooth. Pass through a sieve.

Celeriac Gratin (Prepare the day before)

Bring the cream, garlic and herbs to the boil. Leave to infuse off the heat for 10 minutes before passing through a sieve.

Preheat the oven to 150°C (fan). In your prepared tray, layer the potato with the celeriac and infused cream. Season each layer. Continue layering until two thirds full. Cover with foil and bake for 1 hour 20 minutes. When cooked, press in the fridge overnight with a heavy weight. Cut into 5cm rings.

Duck Crackling

Preheat the oven to 160°C (fan).

Place the duck skin between 2 trays lined with baking paper. Bake for 40 minutes and remove when crispy.

For The Cannelloni

Add the pasta dough ingredients into a blender and pulse together. Rest in the fridge for 20 minutes. Roll the pasta on a machine to number 2, then add the *confit* meat barrel and wrap tightly in cling film. Tie the ends tightly. Poach for 5 minutes, then cut ends to remove.

For The Duck

Preheat the oven to 180°C (fan).

Carefully trim all the excess fat off the breast and score the fat. Caramelise in a hot, ovenproof pan on all sides until golden brown. Cook in the oven for 7 minutes, then leave to rest for 5 minutes.

To Assemble

Swipe the purée using a squeezy bottle. Brush the warm breast in apricot marmalade. Carve the breast in half. Carefully arrange on the plate with all elements of the dish.

VANILLA & GINGERBREAD PANNA COTTA, BABY MERINGUES, STRAWBERRIES & ELDERFLOWER

SERVES 4

🍷 *Errazuriz Late Harvest Sauvignon Blanc (Chile)*

Ingredients

Strawberry Purée

100g strawberries
50g sugar
3 tbsp elderflower cordial

Panna Cotta

1 litre cream
2 tbsp gingerbread essence
2 tbsp vanilla essence
2 leaves gelatine (soaked in cold water)
110g sugar
1 vanilla pod

Shortbread

90g plain flour
60g butter
30g sugar
1 vanilla pod (scraped)
caster sugar (for sprinkling)

Meringues

4 medium egg whites
1 tbsp cornflour
1 tbsp white wine vinegar
75g caster sugar
100g freeze dried strawberries (optional)

Garnish

strawberries

4 metal moulds

Method

To Make The Shortbread

In a food processor, blend the butter, flour, sugar and vanilla seeds to a fine breadcrumb. Add a drop of cold water to bind together, then rest in the fridge. Roll and cut into 15x2.5cm fingers. Rest in the fridge again while heating the oven to 180°C (fan). Bake for 12 minutes, then sprinkle with caster sugar.

For The Strawberry Purée

Combine all the ingredients in a pan and bring to the boil. Reduce to a pulp, blend, then pass through a sieve.

For The Panna Cotta

Split the vanilla pod and scrape all seeds out with a sharp knife. Bring the cream, sugar, vanilla and essences to the boil. Add the gelatine, stir well and place in metal moulds of your choice.

> **Chef's Tip**
> Make the panna cotta 24 hours in advance.

To Make The Meringues

Preheat the oven to 90°C.

Mix all the ingredients together until it forms a soft white cloud, has doubled in volume and is smooth and shiny. On non-stick mats, pipe little meringue dots and dry in the oven for 90 minutes.

Blend the freeze dried strawberries (if using) and sieve over the top of the meringues.

To Serve

Carefully remove the panna cottas from the moulds and serve as pictured.

296
STORRS HALL

Windermere, Cumbria, LA23 3LG

01539 447 111
www.storrshall.com Twitter: @StorrsHall Facebook: www.facebook.com/storrshall

A stunning four star hotel set in 17 acres of grounds on the shores of Lake Windermere.

Amongst all the hotels in the Lake District, Storrs Hall is unquestionably one of the most spectacular. It is surrounded by the natural beauty of the Lake District.

The hotel, a grade II Georgian Mansion, offers an idyllic setting to enjoy a luxury hotel experience. Storrs Hall, with its National Trust-owned folly 'The Temple', has for years been a landmark to sigh over.

Sitting in an unrivalled position, this 30 bedroom lakeland hotel enjoys views of Lake Windermere that seem endless.

The recently refurbished ground floor public interiors create an air of comfort and elegance but retain an informal, warm and welcoming ambiance. At every turn, breathtaking views of lake and fell can be glimpsed through great windows. The luxury bedrooms have huge beds and beautiful bathrooms with every modern convenience.

Conor Toomey, head chef, arrived from the prestigious 2 Michelin, 5 AA Rosette The Latymer at Pennyhill Park, Surrey and more recently Coworth Park, Berkshire where he regained and held the 3 AA Rosette accolade. Conor's ethos and style on the plate is ever progressive but always remains true to delivering exceptional quality, utilising local and seasonal produce to design and craft dishes of memorable notability.

Relish Restaurant Rewards
See page 003 for details.

Conor and his dedicated team enjoying a moment of calm in the gardens of Storrs Hall on the shores of Windermere. Guests are welcome to soak up the relaxed nature that Storrs Hall has to offer and sample some of Conor's decadent treats at leisure within the refurbished public areas of the hotel or in the grounds during the warmer months.

VEAL, BABY BEETROOT, HAZELNUT

SERVES 4

*Luis Felipe Edwards Gran Reserva Merlot 2012
(Colchagua Valley, Chile)*

Ingredients

Beetroot Cooking Liquor

20ml sherry vinegar
15ml red wine vinegar
200ml water
10g sugar
1 star anise
4 sprigs of thyme
1 bunch mixed baby red beetroot

Sweetbread Poaching Liquor

2g tarragon
5 white peppercorns
10g salt
2g thyme
500ml water
350g veal sweetbreads

Golden Beetroot Purée

500g golden beetroot (peeled)
5g salt
125g unsalted butter
10ml smoked oil

Hazelnut Powder

30g maltodextrin
10ml hazelnut oil
8g peeled hazelnuts (toasted, crushed)

Method

For The Beetroot

Combine all the ingredients and add the beetroot to the liquor. Bring to the boil, then simmer gently for approximately 40 minutes. To check if the beetroot is cooked, push a thin blade into the beetroot. If it goes in with little resistance they are done. Run under cold water. Once cool, gently remove the skin by rubbing it off.

For The Sweetbreads

First, peel the membrane around the sweetbreads (if you have a nice butcher he may do this for you). Combine all the ingredients, except the sweetbreads, and bring to the boil. Once at the boil, add the sweetbreads, reduce the heat and simmer for 5 minutes. When done, transfer to a tray and refrigerate immediately. Divide into 4.

> **Chef's Tip**
>
> Always remember to rinse the sweetbread under cold, running water for at least half an hour. This will help remove any excess blood, so when you cook them they are lovely and white.

For The Golden Beetroot Purée

Peel the beetroots whilst raw. Thinly slice then add to a pan on a medium heat with some butter. Sweat until a spoon breaks the beetroot easily. Transfer to a food processor, then blend until smooth.

For The Hazelnut Powder

Put the maltodextrin in a large bowl and slowly add the oil. Whisk continuously until a powder is formed. Finally, incorporate the crushed hazelnuts.

To Serve

Heat a pan with some oil. Colour the sweetbreads in the pan until light golden all round. Place the purée onto the plate, then the sweetbread. Arrange the beetroots and finish with the powder.

COD, ROAST LEEK, POMEGRANATE

SERVES 4

Escarpment The Edge Pinot Gris 2010
(New Zealand)

Ingredients

Salt Cod

1kg cod loin (deboned, scaled)
3g five spice
250g sea salt
2g lime zest
10g fresh coriander

Roast Leek Purée

800g leek tops (the greener the better)
200g unsalted butter
100ml chicken stock

Quinoa Cooking Stock

250ml chicken stock
2g fresh thyme
1 clove garlic
80g black quinoa

Pomegranate Dressing

1 pomegranate (halved)
5g wild honey
50g black quinoa (cooked)
1ml Chardonnay vinegar

Garnish

dandelion
pennywort

Method

For The Salt Cod

Place the cod onto a tray, skin-side down. Combine all the ingredients and rub onto the cod, ensuring that all the flesh is covered. Place the fish into the fridge and allow 30 minutes of salting. Remove from the fridge and gently scrape off the excess salt. Rinse the loin under cold water for 3 minutes. Pat dry and return to the fridge.

> **Chef's Tip**
>
> Cod is not the only fish that benefits from a light salting, try haddock or pollock. Salting helps the fish stay together when cooking, so you keep that lovely shape.

For The Roast Leek Purée

Rinse the leek tops thoroughly, making sure there is no dirt left. Thinly slice the tops. In a heavy bottomed pan, add the butter and allow it to melt. Over a medium heat, add the leeks to the pan. Gently colour the leeks until they start to darken slightly. Remove from the heat. Whilst still hot, place into a food processor and start to blitz. Slowly add the chicken stock until the purée is smooth.

For The Quinoa

Place all the ingredients into a pan. Bring up to the boil and simmer for 12 minutes.

Strain and remove the garlic and thyme.

For The Pomegranate Dressing

To remove the seeds, firmly tap the back of the fruit with a spoon. Combine the honey and vinegar, then add the pomegranate seeds and quinoa.

To Serve

Preheat the oven to 170°C (fan).

Size the cod into 4 equal portions. Place the fish, skin-side down, on a tray and bake in the oven for 7 minutes. Spoon some of the purée onto the plate, then the pomegranate dressing and top with the cod. We garnish with a little salad made from dandelion and pennywort.

PEACH, RASPBERRY SORBET, CUSTARD

SERVES 4

 Château Les Sablines Monbazillac (France)

Ingredients

Stock Syrup

300ml water
300g caster sugar

Raspberry Sorbet

600g raspberry purée
10ml elderflower cordial
150ml stock syrup

Almond Shortbread

170g plain flour
57g ground almonds
85g caster sugar
284g butter

Baked Peach

2 peaches (cut in half, keep the stone in each half)
80g Demerara sugar
40g unsalted butter

Meringue

100g egg whites
(approximately 2½ large egg whites)
100g caster sugar
50g icing sugar

Vanilla Custard

224g sugar
12 egg yolks
560ml double cream

Garnish

fresh raspberries

Method

For The Stock Syrup

Combine the sugar and water then bring to a simmer. Once the liquid becomes clear, remove from the heat. Chill until needed.

For The Sorbet

Combine the purée, cordial and stock syrup in a pan and warm gently. Freeze to set for approximately 4 hours.

For The Shortbread

Preheat the oven to 150°C (fan).

Beat the butter and sugar together, gently work in both the ground almonds and flour.

Roll out to 6mm thick on a lightly floured surface. Bake on a large sheet for 9-11 minutes until golden. Sprinkle with sugar after cooking. Crumble once cooled.

For The Baked Peach

Preheat the oven to 180°C (fan).

Sprinkle the sugar over both halves of the peach with the stone still inside, and divide the butter between both. Bake in the oven for 15-20 minutes. The peach should be slightly caramelised and very soft when done. Allow to cool. Serve at room temperature.

> **Chef's Tip**
> Always take fruit out of your fridge a few hours before serving as the cold of the fridge affects the flavour. Cold fruit does not smell as strong as that at room temperature.

For The Meringue

Preheat the oven to 85°C (fan).

Whisk the egg whites and slowly add the caster sugar. Continue until firm peaks are achieved. Now fold in the icing sugar. Pipe onto greaseproof paper into your desired shape. Bake for approximately 15-20 minutes.

For The Custard

Cream the yolks and the sugar together. Bring the cream to the boil and pour onto the creamed sugar. Add the mix to a clean pan and cook to 82°C, stirring at all times. Once it has thickened enough to coat the back of a spoon, pass through a sieve and refrigerate.

To Serve

Slice the peach halves. Crumble some of the shortbread around your plate. Arrange some slices of the peach on each plate, along with the meringue. Scoop a ball of sorbet, garnish with some fresh raspberries and finish with your custard.

306
THE SUN INN

6 Market Street, Kirkby Lonsdale, LA6 2AU

01524 271 965
www.sun-inn.info Twitter: @suninnkirkbylon

The beautiful market town of Kirkby Lonsdale is in the Lune Valley, where the three counties of Yorkshire, Cumbria and Lancashire meet. Set above the River Lune looking across to Barbon Fell, the view painted by Turner was described by John Ruskin as 'one of the fairest in England and therefore the world'. A town that has everything: riverside walks, picture perfect cottages, cobbled walkways and fabulous shops.

This 17th Century inn has been lovingly restored by Mark and Lucy Fuller over a period of eight years to create a relaxing bar, stylish restaurant and eleven sumptuous rooms.

Sink into a leather cushioned window seat or armchair and toast beside one of the log burners enjoying real ales, a fine selection of wines and a good range for the coffee and tea-o-holic. Care and attention to detail abounds with polished oak floors, original artwork and crystal glasses. The restaurant features handmade furniture courtesy of Lucy's father and dining chairs rescued from the Mauritania.

Friendly service from the loyal team of staff is led by manager Steve Turner. Head chef Sam Carter creates tasty treats from local seasonal ingredients, combining flavours and textures to delight the palate. Enjoy Herdwick hogget from Yew Tree Farm in Cumbria, or salmon and trout from the Argyll Smokery.

Muddy boots and muddy paws welcome.

Relish Restaurant Rewards
See page 003 for details.

Our business is all about people and a special mention must go to our staff. Loving customers is just a natural way of life for our dedicated team. Making people feel comfortable, at home and very much cared for, comes from the heart. It's the small things in life that make it special.

DUCK FRITTER, YORKSHIRE RHUBARB, GINGERBREAD

SERVES 4

 Casa Lapostolle Cabernet Sauvignon (Chile)

Ingredients

Duck Fritter

4 duck legs
150g salt
6 sprigs thyme (picked)
250g duck fat
200ml chicken stock
1 star anise
1 loaf gingerbread
(thinly sliced into 12-15 slices)
1 orange (zest of)
salt (pinch of)

Rhubarb

250g Yorkshire rhubarb (cut into 3cm lengths)
250g sugar
250ml water
vanilla pod

Garnish

rhubarb chard (*sautéed*)

Method

For The Duck Fritter (Prepare at least 10 hours before)

Mix the salt and thyme together and rub all over the duck legs. Leave in the fridge for 6 hours, then thoroughly rinse off the salt.

Preheat the oven to 125ºC. Place the duck legs in a roasting tin and three quarters cover in duck fat. Cook in the oven for 3-4 hours until the meat is falling off the bones. Remove the duck legs from the fat, leave to cool, then pick the meat from the bones.

Add the star anise to the chicken stock and reduce by half over high heat.

Arrange the slices of gingerbread on a baking tray and dry out in the oven at 100ºC for about an hour until crisp. Put 4 slices aside and blitz the rest into crumbs.

Combine the picked duck, reduced chicken stock, orange zest, and a pinch of salt in a bowl. Roll into balls and coat with the gingerbread crumbs.

For The Rhubarb

Split the vanilla pod open and add to a pan with the sugar and water. Bring to the boil, stirring to dissolve all the sugar. Remove from the heat and add the rhubarb. Cover with cling film and leave aside to poach until cool.

Chef's Tip

Poach the rhubarb off the heat otherwise it overcooks.

To Serve

Deep fry the balls of duck until golden. Arrange on plates with pieces of poached rhubarb and slices of gingerbread. Garnish with rhubarb chard.

CHICKEN BOUDIN, SMOKED PORK BELLY, PARISIAN GNOCCHI, ASPARAGUS, WILD GARLIC

SERVES 4

 Meerlust Chardonnay, Stellenbosch (South Africa)

Ingredients

Chicken Boudin

6 chicken breasts
250ml double cream
salt (pinch of)
1 litre chicken stock

Smoked Pork Belly

500g smoked pork belly

Parisian Gnocchi

75g butter (cubed)
175g plain flour
175ml water
salt (to season)
nutmeg (to season)
3 medium eggs
100g Parmesan (grated)

Vegetables

1 bunch asparagus (trimmed)
200g wild garlic leaves, butter (knob of)

To Garnish

1 punnet pea shoots

Method

For The Chicken Boudin

Dice 2 chicken breasts and put in a blender. Slowly add the double cream and a pinch of salt and blend until a mousse consistency is reached. Don't over blend as the cream can split.

Cut the remaining 4 chicken breasts open without cutting through completely (butterfly). Add the mousse in the centre of each breast. Fold over and tightly wrap in cling film, tying with a knot at each end and forming a 'sausage' shape. Chill for 1 hour.

Preheat the oven to 140ºC. Place the chicken breasts into the chicken stock (still in cling film) and cook in the oven for 25 minutes. Take out of the stock and allow to cool. Save some chicken stock for serving.

> **Chef's Tip**
> When making the chicken mousse, add the cream slowly otherwise the mixture will split.

For The Smoked Pork Belly

Preheat the oven to 140ºC.

Place the pork belly on a baking tray and cook in the oven for 2-3 hours until tender. Allow to cool then cut into 2cm cubes.

For The Vegetables

Gently cook the asparagus in salted water until just tender. Toss the wild garlic leaves in butter.

For The Parisian Gnocchi

Melt the butter in a pan, add the flour and cook for 2-3 minutes, stirring constantly. Add the water and keep stirring until thickened. Season with salt and nutmeg. Remove from the heat, put into a mixer and add 1 egg at a time until all is combined. Add the Parmesan and mix until it reaches a dough-like consistency. Turn out the dough, tear off small pieces and roll into balls.

Add the gnocchi balls to boiling water, a few at a time. When they rise to the surface they are cooked. Serve straight away.

To Serve

Preheat the oven to 180ºC.

Remove cling film from the chicken and pan fry gently to lightly colour. Pop in the oven for 5-6 minutes. Cut into 3 to serve. Reheat the pork belly squares in the oven for 5 minutes.

Place the pork belly, chicken, gnocchi, wild garlic and asparagus onto the plate with a little chicken stock. Garnish with pea shoots.

CARROT SPONGE, ORANGE CREAM, CARAMELISED WALNUTS, RAISIN COULIS

SERVES 6 (You can eat the trimmings!)

 *Yalumba Botrytis Viognier
(Australia)*

Ingredients

Carrot Sponge

175g brown sugar
3 medium eggs
175ml sunflower oil
175g self-raising flour
1 tsp bicarbonate of soda
1 tsp cinnamon
½ tsp nutmeg
140g carrots (grated)
100g raisins
orange (zest of)

Orange Cream

200g cream cheese
50g icing sugar
1 orange (zest of)
1 tsp cinnamon

Caramelised Walnuts

50ml water
150g caster sugar
150g walnuts

Raisin Coulis

35ml rum
150g raisins
50g sugar
50ml water

To Serve

orange sorbet
coriander leaves

20cm square cake tin (lined, greased)

Method

To Make The Carrot Sponge

Preheat the oven to 170°C.

Combine the eggs and sugar in a mixer, mix well then add the flour, bicarbonate of soda, sunflower oil, cinnamon and nutmeg. Take out of the mixer and stir in the grated carrots, zest and raisins then mix well. Leave to rest for 10 minutes.

Place in the prepared tin and bake in the oven for 25 minutes.

For The Orange Cream

Combine the cream cheese with the icing sugar, orange zest and cinnamon. Mix until smooth.

For The Caramelised Walnuts

Boil the sugar and water together until it starts to turn white. Add the walnuts, stir quickly to coat and turn out onto greaseproof paper.

> **Chef's Tip**
> Keep an eye on the sugar and water when making the caramelised walnuts to make sure it doesn't burn.

For The Raisin Coulis

Combine the sugar, water, raisins and rum. Boil for 2-3 minutes then blend. Pass through a fine sieve.

To Serve

Cut the carrot sponge into 10cm pieces. Dollop the orange cream onto the plate and spread out using the back of a spoon. Arrange a square of carrot sponge on top. Dribble a few drops of coulis onto the cake and scatter with the caramelised walnuts. Serve with a scoop of sorbet and garnish with coriander leaves.

316

TWELVE RESTAURANT & LOUNGE BAR

Marsh Mill Village, Thornton Cleveleys, Lancashire, FY5 4JZ

01253 82 12 12
www.twelve-restaurant.co.uk Twitter: @twelvethornton Facebook: www.facebook.com/twelvethornton

Chic and contemporary with a modern British menu, Twelve Restaurant and Lounge Bar is located on the Lancashire coast at Marsh Mill Village under the historic 1794 windmill in Thornton Cleveleys. Twelve has an industrial, ultra modern look, with exposed air ducts and beams, brick walls, wooden and slate flooring and designer furniture.

Twelve has been owned and run since 2000 by husband and wife team, Paul Moss and Caroline Upton, who are self-confessed foodies. They have a reputation for creativity and culinary excellence combined with great warmth and geniality and a passion for fine dining and hospitality. Twelve's bold and innovative cooking, using regionally sourced seasonal produce, has brought it critical acclaim and numerous national awards.

Twelve was proudly awarded a Michelin Bib Gourmand in 2005 and has retained it annually since, and the team was further delighted in 2007 to have gained 2 AA Rosettes, which it still maintains.

The restaurant has grown over the years with the outside catering arm of the business now providing its food at iconic venues across Lancashire. Caroline Upton said: 'We owe much to our team who have travelled with us on our journey over the years; the chefs are passionate about developing and experimenting to create exquisite food with exceptional attention to detail, with the front of house team giving a level of service to exceed expectations, although always relaxed'. Currently, chef patron Paul Moss works alongside head chef Graham Floyd as they create dishes that are simply cooked so as to enhance the freshest quality ingredients and ensure every item tastes fabulous.

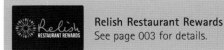

Relish Restaurant Rewards
See page 003 for details.

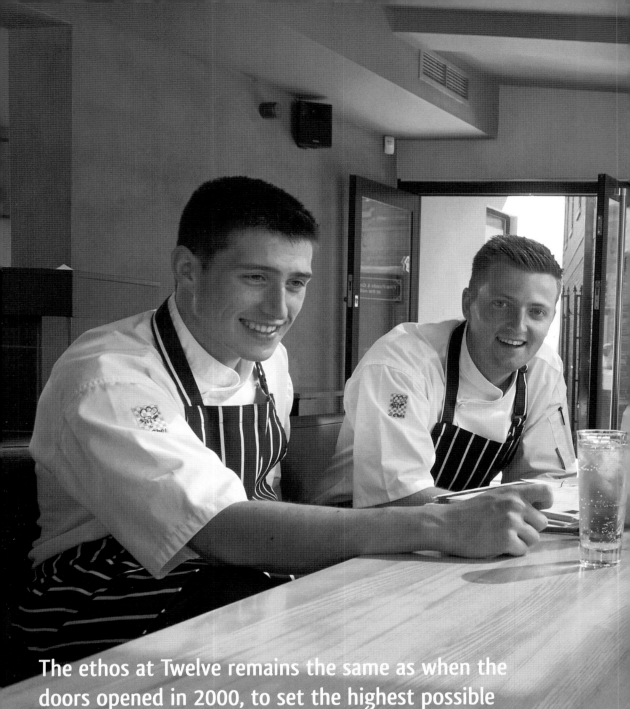

The ethos at Twelve remains the same as when the doors opened in 2000, to set the highest possible standards in catering and hospitality. The aim is always to deliver a flawless organisation, spectacular design, delicious food and drink, delivered by highly personable and professional staff.

GOAT'S CHEESE PANNA COTTA, CANDIED HAZELNUTS, PICKLED BEETROOT

SERVES 4

Albarino Casal Caeiro 2012, Rias Baixas
(Spain)

Ingredients

Goat's Cheese Panna Cotta

300ml double cream
200ml full-fat milk
200g goat's cheese (without rind)
4 bronze gelatine leaves (soaked, excess water squeezed out)

Hazelnuts

100g hazelnuts
100g caster sugar

Pickled Beetroot

500g red beetroot (peeled)
400ml red wine vinegar
400ml water
1 orange (zest of)
2 sprigs thyme
1 tsp coriander seeds
50g sugar

Beetroot Purée

100g pickled cooked beetroot
50ml pickling liquor (taken from pickled beetroot recipe)
5g salt

Beetroot Sorbet

150g sugar
150ml water
440ml beetroot juice
20ml lemon juice
60ml liquid glucose
2 gelatine leaves (soaked in cold water)

Garnish

coriander cress
brioche crisps

4 x A5 sheets acetate

Method

For the Panna Cotta (Prepare the day before)

Heat the milk and cream. Slowly stir in the goat's cheese, then add in the soaked gelatine leaves. Season with salt. Pass the liquid through a sieve and cool in a bowl over ice. Whisk until soft peaks form. Make cylinder tubes from the acetate, approximately 2½cm in diameter and 20cm long. Seal one end by wrapping in cling film. Pour the goat's cheese mix into tubes and set in the fridge for a minimum of 12 hours.

> **Chef's Tip**
> Use a piping bag to pipe the goat's cheese into the acetate tube cylinders. All elements of this dish may be prepared ahead.

For The Hazelnuts

Preheat the oven to 180°C.

Roast the hazelnuts for 10-15 minutes until the skins fall off. Caramelise the sugar in a pan and fold the hazelnuts through the sugar. Leave to cool on a tray and break up into pieces. Keep in an airtight container.

For The Pickled Beetroot

Place all the ingredients into a pan and cook the beetroot in the liquor until soft to bite. Leave to cool. Store the beetroot in the fridge in the pickling liquor.

For The Beetroot Purée

Blitz the 100g of pickled beetroot and the liquor until smooth in a food liquidiser. Season with salt. Pass the liquid through a fine sieve. Refrigerate until needed.

For The Beetroot Sorbet

Place the sugar and water into a pan. Dissolve so that a sugar syrup is produced. Remove from the heat. Add the sugar syrup to the beetroot juice, lemon juice and liquid glucose. Stir in the soaked gelatine leaves. Cool, then churn in an ice cream machine and freeze until set.

To Serve The Dish

Slice the remaining pickled beetroot into wedges and assemble as pictured.

GRESSINGHAM DUCK BREAST, GRANOLA, RAISIN PUREE, YOLK

SERVES 4

Shiraz Deakin Estate 2010
(Australia)

Ingredients

Duck And Skin
4 Gressingham duck breasts (skin reserved)
Maldon salt

4 free range duck eggs (scrubbed, sanitised)

Cabbage And Bacon
100g streaky bacon (chopped)
100ml sherry vinegar
¼ Savoy cabbage (thinly sliced)
100g duck fat

Potato Fondants
2 large Maris Piper potatoes
250g salted butter (sliced)
sprig thyme

Granola
200g almonds
100g pine nuts
1 tsp coriander seeds (toasted, crushed)
4 cloves garlic (sliced)
50ml milk
3 tbsp walnut oil
salt, lemon zest (to taste)

Raisin Purée
250ml dry cider
250g caster sugar
1 stick cinnamon
1 Granny Smith apple (peeled)
1 orange (zest of)
1 star anise, 25g honey, 250g raisins

Red Wine Sauce
vegetable oil (to coat bottom of pan)
1 shallot, 1 carrot, 1 leek (all thinly sliced)
1 clove garlic (crushed)
1 stick celery (thinly sliced)
1 sprig each thyme and rosemary, 1 bay leaf
50ml red wine, 50ml red wine vinegar
100ml port, 500ml brown chicken stock

parchment paper, 2cm round cutter

Method

For The Duck (Prepare the day before)
Wrap the breasts in cling film to form a cylinder shape. Refrigerate for 24 hours. Place the wrapped breasts in a water bath for 1 hour at 54°C, or poach in a pan of water at a slow simmer for 20 minutes. Place the skin on a tray lined with parchment. Season with salt. Cover with parchment and place a baking tray on top. Transfer to a preheated oven at 180°C. Cook for 30 minutes until crispy.

Chef's Tip
Scrape the fat off the back of the duck skin. This will ensure crispy, dried skin.

For The Eggs
Cook the eggs in their shells at 65°C for 1 hour in a water bath. Chill in an ice bath for 30 minutes. Peel the eggs and take the white away from the yolk. Store the yolks in the fridge until required. You may serve this dish without the egg if you do not have a water bath.

For The Cabbage And Bacon
Fry the streaky bacon in the vinegar. Reduce in the pan until sweet and sticky. In a separate pan, *sauté* the cabbage in duck fat until cooked.

For The Fondant Potatoes
Peel and slice the potatoes lengthways into 2cm wide pieces. Cut into 2cm rings. Place the potatoes and thyme on the melting butter and fry until golden. Turn the potatoes over and cook until soft on a low heat for about 15 minutes.

For The Granola
Preheat the oven to 180°C. Roast the almonds and pine nuts on a baking tray for 10 minutes until golden brown. Boil the garlic slices in milk until soft. Drain the slices, then deep fry at 180°C until crisp and golden. Mix all the ingredients together.

For The Raisin Purée
Place all the ingredients (except the raisins) into a pan and reduce by half on a low heat. Add raisins, cook for one minute. Blitz in a liquidizer and sieve. Pour into a bottle and refrigerate until needed.

For The Red Wine Sauce
Heat the oil in a medium sized pan. When smoking, add the vegetables and cook until golden. Add all other ingredients, apart from the stock and reduce until almost dry. Add the stock and reduce by half. Remove from the heat and pass through a fine sieve.

To Serve
Remove the cling film from the breasts and sear in a hot pan with a little oil for 2 minutes to colour. Season, set aside. Reheat the egg yolk under the grill, slice the duck and assemble as pictured.

CREMA CATALANA, SPANISH CHURROS

SERVES 8

 Pineau Des Charentes Château de Beaulon
5 Year Old (France)

Ingredients

Crema Catalana
375ml full-fat milk
125ml double cream
½ lemon (zest of)
½ stick cinnamon, ½ vanilla pod
90g egg yolks (4-5 egg yolks)
45g caster sugar
65g cornflour
60ml water
½ tsp agar agar
½ gelatine leaf (softened in cold water)

Coffee Ice Cream
6 egg yolks
200g granulated sugar
600ml full-fat milk
500ml double cream
4 tsp instant coffee
100g small chunks dark chocolate (melted)

Chocolate Ganache
125ml full-fat milk, 125ml double cream
½ vanilla pod
45g caster sugar
50g egg yolks (2-3 egg yolks)
100g dark chocolate (70% cocoa solids)

Chocolate Sauce
100g dark chocolate (chopped)
50ml double cream
25ml full-fat milk
25g glucose
50ml water

Churros
60g self-raising flour
60g plain flour
225ml water, 1 tbsp oil
80g caster sugar, 1 tsp cinnamon

Garnish
banana (sliced)
brioche crisps
Maldon salt, Demerara sugar

Method

For The Crema Catalana (Allow 3 hours to set)
Bring the cream, milk, lemon zest, cinnamon and vanilla to the boil, then remove from the heat. Allow to infuse for 10 minutes, then strain into a clean bowl. Beat the egg yolks and sugar together, then add the cornflour. Pour the cream mixture over the egg mix, stirring well with a wooden spoon. Bring the water to the boil. Mix in the gelatine and agar agar. Stir into the cream mixture. Strain again. Pour into an isi whipper and charge with 2 gases.

For The Coffee Ice Cream
Whisk the yolks and sugar to a ribbon stage. Bring the milk and cream to the boil, then pour over the yolk and sugar mix. Cook over a *bain marie* to 80°C. Dissolve the coffee into the mix whilst it is still hot, add the chocolate. Chill, then churn in an ice cream machine.

For The Chocolate Ganache (Prepare ahead)
Boil the milk, cream, vanilla and sugar together, then strain the mixture. Add the egg yolks and heat again to 85°C. Mix in the cold chocolate and *emulsify* in a food mixer. Place in a container in the fridge and allow to cool for approximately 8 hours.

For The Chocolate Sauce
Melt the chocolate over a *bain marie*. Boil the cream, milk and glucose, then add to the chocolate. Finish by adding the water.

Chef's Tip
Easy chocolate sauce - melt chocolate, cream and butter in the microwave until it has a runny consistency.

For The Churros
Mix the flours together. Bring the water and oil to the boil and pour over the flour mix to create a wet dough. Rest the mixture for 20 minutes. Place the mixture in a piping bag with a star nozzle. Pipe the mixture in lengths of approximately 5cm directly into a deep fat fryer heated to 180°C, taking care not to splash yourself. Fry the churros until golden brown. Mix the sugar and cinnamon together and roll the hot churros in the flavoured sugar.

To Serve
Arrange a few slices of fresh banana at the bottom of a glass. Coat in chocolate sauce, place a scoop of coffee ice cream into the glass. Dispense the catalana mix from the isi bottle, glaze with Demerara sugar using a blow torch. Spoon the chocolate ganache onto your plates and sprinkle with salt. Arrange the warm cinnamon churros onto the plate and assemble as pictured.

326 WORDSWORTH HOTEL & SPA SIGNATURE RESTAURANT

Stock Lane, Grasmere, Cumbria, LA22 9SW

01539 435 592
www.thewordsworthhotel.co.uk Twitter: @WordsworthHotel Facebook: thewordsworth

Grasmere's Wordsworth Hotel and Spa is a legendary four star hotel in the Lake District.

The hotel is renowned for offering classic luxury in the most beautiful part of the country, serving excellent food with top class service in an historic country house hotel.

Over the last four years, The Wordsworth has been carefully refurbished, retaining its great ambience, character and charm whilst ensuring it has the stylish and luxurious edge travellers expect.

Beautifully set in two acres of riverside gardens, the hotel has amazing views of the mountains and Grasmere Vale, providing the perfect spot to relax, explore or indulge.

The hotel also benefits from relaxing spa facilities with an indoor heated swimming pool, sauna, jacuzzi and sun terrace. Health and beauty treatments are also on offer.

Wordsworth Hotel is an ideal venue for wedding receptions and special occasions with a wide range of defined and bespoke options to make a perfect event.

The Signature Restaurant has been awarded 2 AA Rosettes and offers fine, seasonal dining in a sophisticated ambience, complemented by a specially selected range of wines. The Dove Bistro satisfies the need for good quality, fresh, comfort dishes to look after those clients who prefer a more informal dining experience.

The hotel also offers a beautiful afternoon tea in our lounges and conservatory, along with the opportunity to dine in our stunning gardens.

The kitchen team is directed primarily by the creativity of chefs Jaid Smallman and Martin Frickel.

Relish Restaurant Rewards
See page 003 for details.

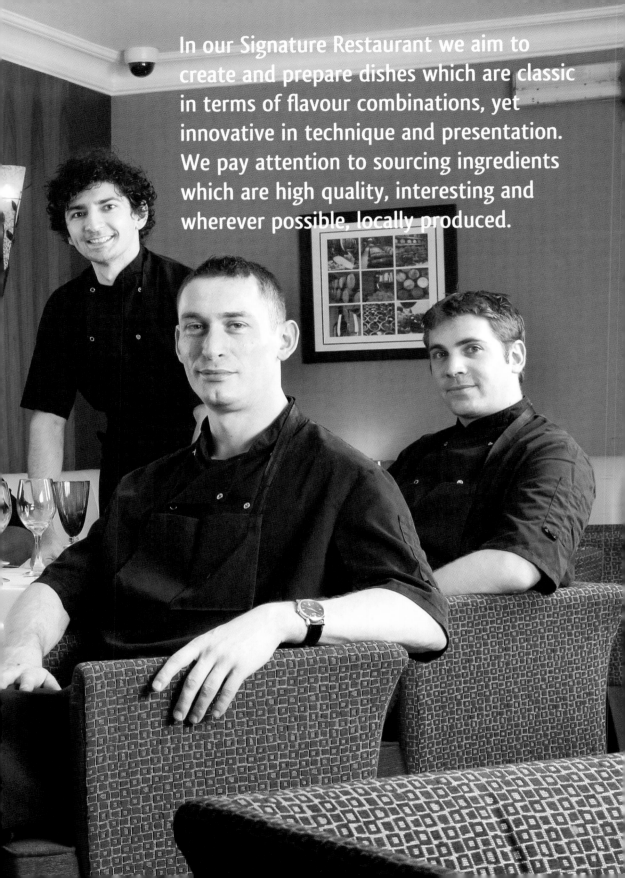

In our Signature Restaurant we aim to create and prepare dishes which are classic in terms of flavour combinations, yet innovative in technique and presentation. We pay attention to sourcing ingredients which are high quality, interesting and wherever possible, locally produced.

RAVENGLASS CRAB CANNELLONI, CUCUMBER, HORSERADISH, PICKLED MACKEREL, NASTURTIUMS

SERVES 4

Verdicchio, Belisario
(Italy)

Ingredients

Crab
200g white crab meat
100g crème fraîche
30g chives (chopped)
20ml white wine vinegar
salt
ground white pepper

Mackerel
1 mackerel (filleted, boned)
200ml white wine
200ml white wine vinegar
200g caster sugar

Cucumber Jelly And Dice
1 cucumber
2g agar agar
1 tbsp mackerel pickling liquor

Horseradish Mayonnaise
50g fresh horseradish (peeled, grated)
2 tbsp mayonnaise

Garnish
8-12 nasturtium leaves
4 nasturtium flowers

20cmx30cm tray (lined with cling film)

Method

For The Crab
Carefully pick through to make sure that there are no remnants of shell. Dress with the crème fraîche and chives. Add white wine vinegar, pepper and salt to taste.

For The Mackerel
Slice the mackerel into 8 pieces. Place the wine, vinegar and sugar in a pan and bring to the boil. Boil steadily until the liquid has reduced by half then cool. Pour this liquor over the mackerel. Reserve a little for the cucumber jelly. Leave to marinate for an hour then drain.

For The Cucumber Jelly And Dice
Peel the cucumber and cut a third of it into 5-7mm slices. Place into a vacuum pouch and compress for 30 seconds. Alternatively, simply cut chunks or slices of cucumber. Blitz the rest of the cucumber in a jug blender, then pass through a fine sieve. Take 180ml of the resultant cucumber juice, add the agar agar and 1 tablespoon of the mackerel pickling liquor, then bring to the boil quickly. Pour out immediately onto the prepared tray so that it forms a very thin layer. Chill until set for approximately an hour.

For The Horseradish Mayonnaise
Add the grated horseradish to the mayonnaise to taste.

To Serve
Spoon a line of the dressed crab meat along the longer edge of the jelly and roll so that the crab is encased. Slice into 4 pieces.

Grill the mackerel pieces, dress the plate with the crab cannelloni, mayonnaise, mackerel and cucumber compression. Garnish with the nasturtium leaves and flowers.

> **Chef's Tip**
> Use cling film to help roll the crab meat in the jelly.

REG JOHNSON'S GOOSNARGH GUINEA FOWL, PEARL BARLEY, HEN OF THE WOODS, CHARRED BABY LEEKS, SPRING CONSOMME

SERVES 4

 Malbec, Bodegas Lagarde
(Argentina)

Ingredients

Guinea Fowl

2 whole guinea fowls
2kg carrots, celery, onion, chestnut mushrooms
and leek (½ roughly chopped by hand, ½ finely
chopped in a food processor)
2 cloves garlic
50g thyme
300ml Madeira
2 litres white chicken stock
6 egg whites
45g tarragon

Turnips And Barley

200g pearl barley
6 baby turnips
20g parsley (finely chopped)
5g tarragon (finely chopped)

Leeks And Mushrooms

8 baby leeks
250g Hen of the Woods (cultivated mushroom)

Method

For The Guinea Fowl And Consommé
(Prepare the day before)

Preheat the oven to 120°C (fan).

Break down the guinea fowl by removing the legs, breasts and livers.

Roast the legs in the oven for 1½ hours. Drain, then flake the meat off the bone. Roast the bones until golden brown. Remove from the roasting tray and dry off any remaining fat. Add the roughly chopped vegetables to a large pan with the garlic and thyme, then fry until browned. Pour in the Madeira and cook until reduced. Add the roasted bones, chicken stock and a little water to cover. Bring this to the boil, skim and simmer gently for up to 6 hours. Pass through a sieve into a new pan and rapidly boil until the flavour is nice and rich. Pour into a wide tray and cool as quickly as possible. When cool, transfer to a fridge overnight.

The next day this will have set into a jelly with any fat set on the surface. Remove all traces of fat from the top. Scoop the rest of the jelly into a saucepan and gently melt, leaving the very bottom layer which contains particles. Mix the egg whites into the finely chopped vegetables. Whisk this into the stock. Slowly increase the temperature until the eggs cook and coagulate with the vegetables at the top of the stock. Carefully sieve the crystal clear stock into another pan. Add the tarragon and seasoning. Reheat when serving.

For The Turnips And Barley

Gently cook the baby turnips and pearl barley in a little of the fowl stock. When cooked, stir in the flaked leg meat and chopped parsley and tarragon.

For The Leeks And Mushrooms

The baby leeks should be *blanched*, refreshed then charred on one side in a frying pan. Add the Hen of the Woods to the same pan.

To Serve

Preheat the oven to 200°C (fan).

Roast the breasts in the oven for 20 minutes. Sear the liver in a hot pan. Arrange the elements of this dish in 4 bowls.

Chef's Tip

Pour the consommé over the dish at the table.

MASCARPONE 'CHEESECAKE', POACHED PEACHES, RASPBERRIES, GRASMERE GINGERBREAD CRUMBLE, MINT

SERVES 4

Late Harvest Semillon & Gewürztraminer, Casa Silva (Chile)

Ingredients

Mousse

1 whole egg
1 egg yolk
85g caster sugar
½ orange (zest of)
¼ vanilla pod
2½ leaves gelatine (soaked in cold water)
250ml whipping cream
250g mascarpone

Raspberry Meringue

200g caster sugar
50ml water
100g egg whites (from 3-4 eggs)
15g freeze dried raspberries

Stock Syrup

¼ vanilla pod
½ orange (zest of)
300g sugar
75ml water

Raspberry Gel

120g raspberry purée
30ml stock syrup
1 tsp Ultratex

Garnish

2 whole fresh peaches (halved, stones removed)
2 pieces Grasmere gingerbread
20 fresh raspberries
micro mint cress

20x30x5cm tray (lined with cling film for the mousse)
20x30cm tray (lined with greaseproof paper for the meringue)

Method

For The Mousse

Put the egg and yolk, sugar, orange zest and vanilla in a bowl and whisk over a pan of boiling water until thick and pale. Whisk in the gelatine. Whip the cream, then fold into the mascarpone whilst the egg mixture is cooling. Fold the cooled egg mix and mascarpone mix together, then place into a tray lined with cling film. Set in the fridge for at least 1½ hours.

For The Meringue

Add the sugar and water to a pan and bring up to 116°C. As the temperature is getting near, whisk the egg whites until soft peaks form, then gradually add the boiling sugar. Continue to whisk until the mixture has cooled. Pour out onto an oven tray lined with greaseproof paper. Crush the freeze dried raspberries and scatter over the surface of the meringue. Dehydrate in the oven on the lowest setting until hard and crisp.

For The Stock Syrup

Put the sugar, water, orange zest and vanilla in a pan and bring to the boil, sieve and cool.

For The Peaches

Place in a pan with the stock syrup (reserve 30ml for the gel). Cook gently for 30 minutes until tender. Drain then cool.

For The Gel

Blend the raspberry purée with the stock syrup and Ultratex until thick and smooth.

To Serve

Crush the gingerbread using a pestle and mortar. Cut the mousse into squares, break the meringue into shards and slice the peaches into lengths for serving. Arrange on plates, garnishing with the gel, raspberries and mint cress.

Chef's Tip

If you do not have a dehydrator you could use an oven on the lowest possible setting.

NORTH WEST LARDER

WELLOCKS
4 Pendleside, Lomeshaye Business Village,
Lancashire, BB9 6SH
T: 08444 993 444
www.wellocks.co.uk

Founded 62 years ago and suppliers of quality vegetables, fruit and a range of dairy and bakery products mainly sourced from local producers and farms.

OLIVER KAY PRODUCE
Produce House, Britannia Way, Bolton, BL2 2HH
T: 08448 479 790
www.oliverkayproduce.co.uk

Fruit and vegetable suppliers and speciality foods.

CARTMEL VALLEY GAME SUPPLIES AND SMOKEHOUSE
High Bankside, Cark-In-Cartmel, Grange-Over-Sands,
Cumbria, LA11 7NR
T: 01539 536 413
E: enquiries@cartmelvalleygamesupplies.com

Cartmel Valley Game nestles in the picturesque historical Cartmel Valley, where Jonathan and Susan run their successful game business from their beautiful Lake District based home. They work closely with their team of highly qualified and dedicated staff, supplying the best quality gourmet game and smoked products to top class establishments.

J & S GOOSNARGH LTD
Johnson and Swarbrick, Swainson House Farm, Goosnargh,
Preston, Lancashire, PR3 2JU
T: 01772 865 251
E: info@jandsgoosnargh.co.uk

Situated on the edge of the Ribble Valley, in the picturesque village of Goosnargh, Johnson and Swarbrick have been producing fine poultry products for the past 3 decades.

PROCTORS CHEESE LTD
The Cheese Warehouse, Saunders Raikem Chipping,
Nr Preston, Lancashire, PR3 2QR
T: 0199 561 626

The Proctor family has been making cheese in the picturesque village of Chipping since the 1930's and the company is now run by the fourth generation of Proctors. The local farms have lush pastures which ensures the production of excellent milk for cheese making.

LUNYA
18-20 College Lane, Liverpool, L1 3DS
T: 0151 706 9770
www.lunya.co.uk

The wines and specialist meats and spices used in Lunya's recipes, pages 166-175, are available in store, or online.

DELIFONSECA
Dockside, Brunswick Quay, Brunswick Way,
Liverpool, L3 4BN
T: 0151 255 0808

Delifonseca's food hall sells all the components of the dishes in the recipes on pages 106-115. These include Cheshire Smokehouse smoked duck breast, pomegranate molasses and samphire in season.

337
GLOSSARY

AL DENTE
Al dente describes vegetables that are cooked to the 'tender crisp' phase - still offering resistance to the bite, but cooked through. Al dente can also describe cooked pasta which is firm but not hard.

BAIN MARIE
A pan or other container of hot water with a bowl placed on top of it. This allows the steam from the water to heat the bowl so ingredients can be gently heated or melted.

BLANCH
Boiling an ingredient before removing it and plunging it in ice cold water in order to stop the cooking process.

BRUNOISE
A type of culinary cut in which food is diced into $1/8$ inch (3.175 mm) cubes. The formal-looking little squares add colour and elegance to dishes.

CARTOUCHE
A round piece of greaseproof paper that covers the surface of a stew, soup, stock or sauce to reduce evaporation.

CHIFFONADE
A chopping technique in which herbs or leafy green vegetables (such as spinach and basil) are cut into long, thin strips.

CHINOIS
A conical sieve with an extremely fine mesh. It is used to strain custards, purées, soups and sauces, producing a very smooth texture.

CONFIT
A method of cooking where the meat is cooked and submerged in a liquid to add flavour. Often this liquid is rendered fat. Confit can also apply to fruits - fruit confits are cooked and preserved in sugar, the result is like candied fruits.

DARIOLE
A French term that refers to small, cylinder shaped moulds.

DEGLAZE
A fancy term for using the flavour-packed brown bits stuck to the bottom of a pan to make a sauce or gravy.

EMULSION/EMULSIFY
In the culinary arts, an emulsion is a mixture of two liquids that would ordinarily not mix together, like oil and vinegar.

FLAMBE
A cooking procedure in which alcohol is added to a hot pan to create a burst of flames

JULIENNE
A culinary knife cut in which the vegetable is cut into long thin strips, similar to matchsticks.

JUS
The natural juices given off by the food.

MACERATED
Raw, dried, or preserved fruit and vegetables soaked in a liquid to soften the food or to absorb the flavour.

MANDOLIN
A cooking utensil used for slicing and for cutting juliennes. Slices can be very thin, and be made very quickly. It ensures that all slices are uniform.

MIREPOIX
Finely diced combination of celery (pascal, celery or celeriac), onions and carrots. There are many regional mirepoix variations, which can sometimes be just one of these ingredients, or include additional spices creating a rich, flavoursome base to sauces or stews.

MONTE
To emulsify with butter, usually used to finish a sauce.

PATE A BOMBE
A pâte à bombe is the French term for a mixture used as a base for making chocolate mousse and other mousse-like desserts.

QUENELLE
A finely minced fish or meat mixture formed into small portions, poached in stock and served in a sauce, or as a garnish to other dishes. The term is also used to describe their characteristic shape - a neat, three-sided oval (resembling a mini rugby ball) that is formed by gently smoothing the mixture between two dessert spoons. A quenelle shape can also be formed from other foods such as chocolate mousse.

SABAYON
Made by beating egg yolks with a liquid over simmering water until thickened and increased in volume. The liquid can be water, but Champagne or wine is often used.

SAUTE
To fry in a small amount of fat.

Relish PUBLICATIONS

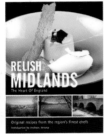

  Download your FREE sample pages now from the App Store/Relish Cookbook.

BEST OF BRITISH

Relish Publications is an independent publishing house offering an exclusive insight into Britain's finest restaurants and chefs through their series of award-winning recipe books.

Each book contains signature recipes from your favourite chefs, recommended wines, stunning food photography and an impressive guide to each participating restaurant, plus a larder featuring the region's best produce suppliers. These ingredients make the Relish series an ultimate 'foodies' guide for individuals wishing to dine in great restaurants or create outstanding recipes at home.

The series of beautiful hard back recipe books is available to buy in the featured restaurants, all good bookshops and online at the Relish bookshop or on Amazon.

For more information please visit **www.relishpublications.co.uk**

Relish PUBLICATIONS

Duncan and Teresa Peters founded Relish Publications in 2009, through a passion for good food, a love of publishing and after recognising the need to promote the fantastic chefs and restaurants each region in the UK has to offer.
Relish Publications also specialise in bespoke cookbooks for individual chefs.

Since launching, their goal was simple. Create beautiful books with high quality contributors (each edition features a selection of the region's top chefs) to build a unique and invaluable recipe book.

As recipe book specialists, their team works with hundreds of chefs personally to ensure each edition exceeds the readers' expectations.

Thank you for Relishing with us!

HERE'S WHAT SOME OF BRITAIN'S BEST CHEFS HAVE SAID ABOUT WORKING WITH RELISH

"The Relish team has truly been amazing to work with. To have produced my book within two months from start to finish, only shows how professional a team of people can be."
Jean-Christophe Novelli

"The Relish cookbook offers the home cook some great inspiration to make the most of these wonderful ingredients in season." *Tom Kitchin, The Kitchin, Edinburgh*

"With mouth-watering, easy to follow recipes and beautiful photography, this book is a must have for any foodie, from professional chef to the inspired home cook."
Michael Caines MBE

"Relish brings together some of the most talented chefs from the regions. It shines the spotlight on the exceptional ways in which fresh, seasonal, local ingredients are put to good use." *Gary Jones, Executive Head Chef, Le Manoir aux Quat'Saisons*

CONVERSION CHART

COOKING TEMPERATURES

Degrees Celsius	Fahrenheit	Gas Mark
140	275	1
150	300	2
160-170	325	3
180	350	4
190	375	5
200-210	400	6
220	425	7
230	450	8
240	475	9

*Temperatures for fan-assisted ovens are, as a general rule, normally about 20°C lower than regular oven temperature. In this book, all temperatures stated are for conventional (non-fan) ovens, unless otherwise specified.

WEIGHT MEASUREMENT CONVERSIONS

1 teaspoon (5ml/5g)	$^1/_4$ oz
1 tablespoon (15ml/15g)	$^3/_4$ oz
10g	$^1/_2$ oz
25g	1oz
50g	2oz
75g	3oz
150g	5oz
200g	7oz
250g	9oz
350g	12oz
450g	1lb
1kg	2.2lb

VOLUME MEASUREMENT CONVERSIONS

55ml	2 fl oz
150ml	$^1/_4$ pt
275ml	$^1/_2$ pint
570ml	1 pt
1 litre	$1^3/_4$ pt